GREAT WALKS
OF NEW ZEALAND

To Mum

Something for a planner to
consider!

Happy mothers day

GREAT WALKS
OF NEW ZEALAND

CRAIG POTTON
WITH SHAUN BARNETT

pb potton & burton

AUCKLAND ●

● Gisborne

Ruapehu
2797m

Mt Taranaki
2518m

Lake Waikaremoana Track
(Te Urewera)

Abel Tasman Coast Track
(Abel Tasman National Park)

Tongariro Northern Circuit
(Tongariro National Park)

Heaphy Track
(Kahurangi National Park)

● Nelson

● WELLINGTON

Hokitika ●

CHRISTCHURCH ●

Aoraki/Mt Cook
3754m

Mt Aspiring
3027m

Milford Sound

Milford Track
(Fiordland National Park)

Routeburn Track
(Fiordland/Mount Aspiring
National Parks)

Lake Wakatipu

Kepler Track
(Fiordland National Park)

Lake Te Anau

Lake Manapouri

● DUNEDIN

● Invercargill

Rakiura Track
(Rakiura National Park)

STEWART ISLAND

CONTENTS

INTRODUCTION

When *Classic Walks of New Zealand* first appeared in 1997, it was the fulfillment of a long-held wish to produce a book celebrating walking in the wilderness. Forests, mountain ranges, rivers and the coast have been a second home for my imagination ever since my adolescence in Nelson when, with close friends, I began exploring the backcountry and discovered a world that not only delighted me but was also much in need of our active care and attention. Natural landscapes speak to us with a powerful voice and, over the years, I have become convinced that the mere act of walking in nature is wonderfully therapeutic. On multi-day tramps, for reasons I can't explain, I find the rhythms of the wild soothe many of my anxieties—I think clearer and sleep with fewer demons tormenting my mind.

This fully revised edition focuses on New Zealand's eight Great Walks, tracks that are well known and popular. I am aware that producing this book will encourage more people to visit these exquisite places, and thereby contribute to their overcrowding and a corresponding loss of space and solitude. However, I can also empathise with the insight of the painter Colin McCahon who described our wilderness as a 'land with too few lovers'. By bringing images of these places into the living room, I hope that something of their wildness or unfamiliarity will trigger a memory, create an abstract joy or spur readers to once more get out and experience nature. I'm sure it is our hearts that lead our heads to such places, and our memories and desires that send us back again and again. For these outstanding tracks pass through landscapes so appealing and diverse that you *do* want to revisit them—in different seasons, accompanied by different people or in different stages of your life.

My intention was not to produce a guide that explains routes and human or natural history in any great detail—many other good publications focus on these goals. Instead I have aimed, through photos and words, to describe what I see and feel on these walks, and evoke something of the value of these places (with the occasional diversion into scientific or personal anecdotes behind the vista).

New Zealand boasts some 13,000 kilometres of public tracks on conservation land, but the Great Walks presented here consistently appear on everyone's 'to do' list. Having no illusions about the severity of much of the landscape or the intensity of the weather, these well-known Great Walks are, without exception, well-constructed and better-serviced lines through the forest, coast and mountains. Compared to many other multi-day tracks, they provide relatively easy passages through the surrounding wilderness.

Many of these walks attract large numbers of people during peak periods, and measures such as hut bookings have been introduced to ensure that the wilderness experience is

Forward Peak, Kepler Track, Fiordland National Park

not unduly compromised. Further, I would be roasted by my conscience (and friends!) if I promoted areas that remain off the beaten track.

There have been times, perhaps after a long day in the wilderness with darkness falling, rain bucketing down and my shoulders in agony from a pack that has got heavier all day, when a hut has come into view, meaning a warm brew of sweet tea, a meal and a soft bunk. At times like this I feel much gratitude to the Department of Conservation workers who maintain these shelters, as well as the other facilities that make it possible to experience a different milieu to the towns and cities in which most of us live.

RAKIURA TRACK

If anywhere gives an impression of what the early settlers must have seen and felt when they first arrived in New Zealand, perhaps it is Stewart Island/Rakiura. On Rakiura the forest is all-encompassing, often stretching right to the sea's edge, and draping all but the higher mountains, dunelands and larger wetlands. In many places there is a sylvan beauty to the forest, especially where stately rimu dominate, but also an overwhelming sense of nature's dominance. Such dense forests, with so few natural clearings, must have seemed oppressive indeed to European settlers more used to bucolic, rural landscapes. As one Scottish settler at Port William noted, 'We can't live on beauty. It won't fill the porridge pot.'

Port William, a sheltered harbour that local Māori knew as Potirepo, today offers trampers a place of tranquility. A gentle sea laps the sandy shore, and the headlands are soft and rounded, with none of the western side of Rakiura's craggy, wave-assaulted shoreline. But this sense of peace belies the struggle and wretchedness of early settlers who had to get to grips with the forest and damp climate. Other than the simple joy of walking through bush and along coastlines, perhaps that is the most compelling reason to undertake the Rakiura Track—to appreciate how the forest wilderness on Stewart Island persisted, despite all efforts to tame it.

Rakiura's current wild state is partly due to its isolation, but the island has a surprisingly long history of attempts to exploit its natural resources. Along the course of the Rakiura Track lies the evidence of past occupation by successive waves of people: first Māori, then whalers and sealers, saw-millers, boat-builders, gold prospectors and settlers. Few found much fortune on the island, and in the end the bush and sea claimed back most of their efforts. What remains, however, adds much of interest.

Despite being New Zealand's third largest island, Stewart Island has only about 20 kilometres of road, all of them radiating from Halfmoon Bay, the island's only town. The remainder of the 168,000-hectare island is road-less and largely uninhabited. In 2002, 85 per cent of the island became New Zealand's fourteenth national park.

Roughly coinciding with the park's formation, the Department of Conservation upgraded previously existing trails to form the Rakiura Track, the most recently developed of New Zealand's Great Walks. It connects the coastline north of Halfmoon Bay with the northern part of Paterson Inlet/Whaka ā Te Wera, forming a tidy triangle beginning and ending near Halfmoon Bay. The two to three-day tramp offers a gentler alternative to the infamous and much more demanding Northwest Circuit.

The track begins five kilometres north of Halfmoon Bay, at Lee Bay, the main entrance to the national park. Here, a

OPPOSITE Coastal scenery between Lee Bay and Port William, near Māori Beach ROBYN CORMACK/DOC

giant chain sculpture spans the track, symbolising the island's alternative name of Te Puka a te Waka a Māui (the anchor stone of Māui's canoe). According to Māori legend, Rakiura is the anchor that secured the waka of demigod Māui when he fished up the North Island.

At first the track sidles through forest dominated by mānuka and kāmahi, with glimpses of the rocky shoreline in several places. The well-benched track is—unlike the vast majority of those on the rest of the island—well drained. While the surface can be a little hard on your feet (wearing light, comfortable boots is preferable to heavy-duty ones) the compensation is a good walking surface—unlike the infamous mud most other Stewart Island tracks are known for. This offers considerable opportunities to observe your surroundings, not just your feet. You might see kākāriki wafting over the canopy, hear the guttural croak of kākā (New Zealand's endemic bush parrot) or watch a fantail flitting through the trees in its search for insects.

At Little River, the track descends to the shoreline to cross a footbridge over a tidal inlet where, like many bays at Stewart Island, pods of pilot whales occasionally strand. Whalers and sealers were some of the first Pākehā attracted to Stewart Island, led by John Grono, who named the sheltered harbour at Port William after his patron, a New South Wales businessman. By 1850, Captain John Howell had established a whaling station in the area. He was later followed by Irish whaler Paddy Gilroy, skipper of a boat called the *Chance,* which regularly plied the waters of Foveaux Strait. Gilroy was once described as 'a queer little figure of a man, short and tubby with a brogue as thick as pea-soup … Overflowing with human kindness and good temper, his ship was a veritable ark of refuge for any unfortunate who needed help.' Not so fortunate were the whales.

Beyond Little River, the track strikes inland until rounding Peters Point, where a tiny island, lying just offshore, is visible

through crooked limbs of pole mānuka. The track descends to the edge of Māori Beach (so named because it has been home to a succession of tiny Māori communities) and the first decent stretch of walking along the sand. Among the mānuka fringing the beach is a pleasant campsite, with a shelter and toilet.

From the campsite, a ten-minute side track leads to an old boiler, the remains of a timber milling venture in the area that spanned a couple of decades during the first part of the twentieth century. Rimu was the main timber sought. The northeastern parts of Rakiura, including Port William, had an abundance of the tall tree, also known as red pine, distinctive because of its khaki-coloured foliage that droop in long sprays. By 1920, the Māori Beach community boasted enough families for a school to open, although it didn't operate on Wednesdays. On that day, the children walked the 12 kilometres to Halfmoon Bay to arrange stores for their families, and caught the boat back with the supplies. The timber at Māori Bay was not inexhaustible, however, and by 1931 the area was once again abandoned.

Tidal inlets exist at the mouth of most streams and rivers at Stewart Island. Fortunately the stream that flows into Wooding Bay, at the western end of Māori Beach, is narrow enough to be spanned by a wooden footbridge; otherwise it would be a long walk around the inlet at high tide.

By now, Magnetic Beach, where Port William Hut is situated, has been visible across the curve of the harbour for some time, but to reach it the track heads inland and climbs about 100 metres to avoid coastal cliffs. Past a signposted junction, the track to Port William Hut begins a gradual descent through some fine rimu, with tree ferns jostling for light in the understorey.

At low tide, it's pleasant to wander along Magnetic Beach,

OPPOSITE Māori Beach and Wooding Bay are reached after Peters Point, en route to Port William Hut PETR HLAVACEK

perhaps even kicking off your boots to let the sand massage your feet. The hut lies beyond a jetty, set in a grassy depression where several large eucalypt trees tower above the surrounding forest. These exotic gums are symbols of a failed endeavour to settle Stewart Island with Scots. In 1871, the Otago Provincial Government decided that Port William would make an ideal location for settlers. Taking no heed that recent attempts to establish an oyster industry and gold mining had both failed, the government decided that the settlers would build houses and boats, grow vegetables and fish the bountiful ocean. Walter Person, the Commissioner of Crown Lands and main architect of the proposed settlement, wrote—rather optimistically—that 'Stewart Island is [so] singularly favourably situated for the proper class of settlers, that it is difficult to determine what they could NOT do.'

The government promised support, and did as much as building large wooden barracks, suitable for up to 150 people, and supplying the first year's worth of food at cost. In 1873, 24 Shetland Islanders, mainly poor crofters and including 11 children, moved into the barracks at Port William—accommodation they found cold and drafty compared to their former cosy cottages.

Like many others who were enticed to New Zealand with overblown promises, the Shetland Islanders were dismayed at the wildness of their surroundings at Port William. But they set to work regardless, laboured to clear the forest, built their own cottages, planted fruit trees and bushes and attempted to establish a fishing industry. However their first three boatloads of fish, sent to Bluff, disappeared with no payment in return. Declining government support, no school or medical services, and despondency at the damp nature of the island led to despair. One settler later recalled 'The hills seemed to huddle together and shake their fists at us.' The violin of one settler 'gave up

singing' in the damp, and from then on hung useless on the wall of his cottage. 'Shetland Island cheerfulness', wrote one historian, 'turned into Port William moroseness.' Within a year, all the settlers had dispersed to the mainland, losing their land, savings and sense of adventure.

The cottages and barracks fell into ruin, and now the site is occupied, rather more usefully, by the present tramping hut. Aside from the grassy clearing, it's only the eucalypts that remain as testimony to the efforts of those poor Shetland Islanders.

After departing Port William, the track to North Arm crosses a forested ridge that separates Foveaux Strait and Paterson Inlet. It is a day of several hours enclosed in the forest, with little to relieve the eye from the enclosing greenery, and virtually nothing in the way of views. The absence of beech and other common mainland trees like mountain toatoa, pāhautea and kōwhai makes Stewart Island's forests seem unfamiliar. The rusty tones of rimu, the conglomerate trunks of kāmahi, sprawling southern rātā and the solid scalloped and flaking trunks of miro mix with other podocarps. Indeed, even for the tramper who enjoys forest rambles, the bush here can seem dark, tangled and rather forbidding, especially in heavy rain—when even at midday it feels like dusk.

Soon after an initial climb, the track reaches on old milling site, where two log haulers lie abandoned—remnants of the Māori Beach settlement. Both are in remarkably good condition thanks to restoration work by DOC archaeologists and volunteers. It is one of several sites on the Rakiura Track where DOC has installed excellent panels explaining the area's history. This one details the ingenuous efforts used to wrest

OPPOSITE Ferns and rimu trunks on the Rakiura Track near Port William
SHAUN BARNETT/BLACK ROBIN PHOTOGRAPHY
OVERLEAF Rātā and rimu forest above Paterson Inlet's North Arm ANDRIS APSE

12

Low tide at North Arm Hut SHAUN BARNETT/BLACK ROBIN PHOTOGRAPHY

At its exposed coastal margins, the forest throws out strange surprises, with large groves of leafy wind- and salt-tolerant shrubs such as *Olearia* and *Brachyglottis*, or tight spiny-leaved *Dracophyllum* shrubs, cuffed into stunted shapes by the prevailing wind. The hut verandah offers a pleasant place to watch the sunset over the Thomson Range on the far side of the inlet.

Like Port William, North Arm has seen considerable human activity, but here more lasting. Several mills operated with some success between the 1860s and 1930s. John Bullock established a mill in 1861 at what became known as Sawdust Bay, and cut so much timber that the resulting sawdust, flushed into the inlet, polluted the waters and temporarily killed all the sea life. In 1870 another mill opened at North Arm.

The last day of the Rakiura Track completes the third side of the triangle back to Halfmoon Bay, skirting the shores of Paterson Inlet en route. In essence it follows old logging roads. At first, pleasantly fringed by ferns and nicely graded, it meanders inland through forest to emerge at Sawdust Bay. Here, granite boulders project out of the sea. On a good day it is a sublime spot, the waters of Paterson Inlet rippling in the breeze and clouds scudding overhead. It is a place where you might experience a day when, as Rakiura-born writer Sheila Natusch once wrote, 'the Island seems to float; distant shores turn up at the edges, low land runs to dissolving blobs and dots of refraction [with] vanishing and reappearing shores'.

Beyond Sawdust Bay, the track climbs over a ridge to reach Kidney Fern Arm, where the pioneer saw-miller William Gallon set up business in 1861. Here are the remains of an earthen dam, once used to operate the mill's waterwheel. Workers extracted enough timber to build three ships in the Kaipipi area, the largest of them a 149-ton, three-masted schooner. However, just as at Māori Beach, the accessible timber ran out and in 1929 the last mill closed. It's always slightly unfathomable that

timber from the forest; one hauler pulled felled trunks out of the bush while the other lowered the logs to the tramway on the beach. It was hard and sometimes dangerous work.

Aside from that historical interlude, the rest of the day's walking is mainly a plod through stunted forest, with only the occasional footbridge over a stream to relieve the monotony. The day's walk does serve the vital function, however, of connecting the coastal sections of the track. Nevertheless, reaching the coast once again at North Arm comes as something of a relief.

North Arm Hut occupies a terrace above a tidal arm of Paterson Inlet, the largest of Stewart Island's several harbours. From the hut, a set of stairs leads to the shore, where at low tide it is possible to scramble around the shore over mussel-encrusted boulders to another tiny bay.

Looking out over Paterson Inlet from the Rakiura Track PETR HLAVACEK

in such places so much activity occurred for decades, but now they are closed in by fern and tree with the sun shut out and nature ruling verdantly once again.

At the main Kaipipi Bay, a 20-metre-long footbridge crosses a tidal inlet, and a few hundred metres further on, a side track leads down to a grassy viewpoint overlooking Burial Island.

The remainder of the walk is easy, undulating travel on a wide section of track once called the 'main road' by the island-ers. Sections of corduroy remain, reminders that this road was once plied often enough to churn it into a quagmire. 'Roads, do you call them?', one visitor to Rakiura quipped. 'I'd say they were mud-pies.'

The Rakiura Track ends at the Fern Gully carpark, where trampers usually walk the short section of road to Halfmoon Bay. For a pleasant alternative, take the Ryans Creek Track. This largely hugs the shoreline, with views of the Hope, Faith and Charity islands. Hope and faith seem appropriate names for the generations of people who have tried to forge an exis-tence at this isolated place in the path of the Roaring Forties. In the end, despite all attempts by humans to tame it, it was the forest that persisted.

—*Shaun Barnett*

MASON BAY TRACK, STEWART ISLAND

For trampers with more time, a wonderful add-on to the Rakiura Track is a return trip out to Mason Bay. Mason Bay is the longest beach at Stewart Island, a 14-kilometre-long arc of sand, backed by an expanse of huge dunes, and one of the larg-est areas of its kind in New Zealand. Near the bay, a trampers' hut occupies a patch of mānuka, set back from the beach, an area well known for its resident population of Rakiura tokoeka/southern brown kiwi, which are often observed during the day.

From North Arm Hut it is a 6–7 hour walk to Freshwater Hut or alternatively you can get a water taxi from Halfmoon Bay to Freshwater Landing. From here it is a day's tramp across swamp and tussock, and through corridors of mānuka, to reach Mason Bay Hut.

The mountainous dunes, ranging some three kilometres inland, and reaching up to 200 metres in height, so impressed early naturalist Herbert Guthrie-Smith that he described Mason Bay as 'space illimitable'. Formerly, many of the dunes were clothed in introduced marram grass, but control efforts in recent years have allowed the native sand-binding plants pingao and *Spinifex* to make a comeback. Pingao roots, stems and leaves bind and surround six-metre peaked dunes, then appear to die back into hairy black skeletons as the sand moves on.

It's a place to wander nowhere slowly; wind sweeps sand away from shallow chasms, leaving strange moonscapes of clay with small pebbles and stones placed like marbles in V-formations.

Long walks on the beach are well worth taking an extra day over. Northwards leads to a boulder bank of wave-smoothed rocks, while to the south lies a narrow inlet between the main beach and the Ernest Islands. Huge southerly swells pulse waves through the eye of this enclosure, named appropriately and without sentiment, 'The Gutter'. Within just 100 metres, sea cliffs rise high above a delicate shell-strewn beach and there is another wave-lashed boulder bank and a shipwreck in the final stages of disintegration.

OPPOSITE Looking north along the sand dunes at Mason Bay ROB BROWN

RAKIURA TRACK
Rakiura National Park, Stewart Island

DISTANCE 32 km

TIME REQUIRED 2–3 days

NEAREST TOWN Halfmoon Bay

BEST TIME TO WALK THE TRACK
October–April

FITNESS Moderate fitness is required

ACCOMMODATION Huts and campsites
must be booked online in advance.
Port William and North Arm huts cost $22
per night. Campsites ($6 per night) exist
near both huts, as well as at Māori Beach.

APPROXIMATE WALKING TIMES
Halfmoon Bay to Lee Bay via Halfmoon
Bay Road
5 kilometres, 1 hour

Lee Bay to Port William Hut
(24 bunks, wood stove)
8 kilometres, 2–3 hours

Port William Hut to North Arm Hut
(24 bunks, wood stove)
13 kilometres, 4–5 hours

North Arm Hut to Halfmoon Bay
11 kilometres, 3.5–4 hours

MASON BAY TRACK (NOT ON MAP)
Rakiura National Park, Stewart Island

LENGTH 15 km (each way)

TIME REQUIRED 2–3 days

NEAREST TOWN Halfmoon Bay

BEST TIME TO WALK THE TRACK
October–April

FITNESS Moderate fitness is required

ACCOMMODATION Freshwater Hut (16
bunks) and Mason Bay Hut (20 bunks)
cost $5 per night, and do not need to be
booked in advance.

APPROXIMATE WALKING TIMES
Freshwater Landing to Mason Bay Hut,
15 km, 3–4 hours. Be aware that the track
can be flooded after heavy rain.

FURTHER INFORMATION
DOC Rakiura National Park Visitor Centre
15 Main Road, Halfmoon Bay
PO Box 3, Stewart Island 9846
Tel: 03 219 0009

Book online at: www.doc.govt.nz
email: greatwalksbooking@doc.govt.nz
or tel: 0800 694 732

Foveaux Strait

Port William Hut

Magnetic Beach

Port William / Potirepo

Peters Point

Wooding Bay

Māori Beach

Lee Bay

Little River

START

Horseshoe Bay

Fern Gully carpark

END

HALFMOON BAY (OBAN)

Ryans Creek Track

Faith, Hope & Charity Group

Kaipipi Bay

Kidney Fern Arm

st Bay

Paterson Inlet / Whaka ā Te Wera

KEPLER TRACK

Of all the Great Walks in this book, the Kepler is the only one that was deemed 'a classic' from the moment it was conceived. Opened in 1988, it came about when the Department of Conservation joined several infrequently used routes on the Kepler Mountains to make a well-constructed track, with the aim of easing the number of walkers crowding onto the Milford and Routeburn tracks. That it failed in this intention and instead offered another high-standard multi-day track to walk in this wonderful part of New Zealand was entirely predictable. But its popularity seems to prove that a track doesn't have to be an ancient Māori greenstone trail or a place of colonial history, or even feel the decades-old reverberations of explorers, hunters, trampers and their ilk to have poignancy in a world overwhelmed by humans.

The well-conceived Kepler Track cuts a daring line across some spectacular Fiordland tops and links many disparate natural features—caverns of limestone, meadows of alpine plants, forests of lowland beech and two lakes of monumental size. Furthermore, it neatly returns to its start at Te Anau like a giant uroboros (the serpent of creation that swallowed its own tail), having led you across a wild edge of Fiordland. It takes between three and four days to walk its 60 kilometres, and can be done clockwise or, as described here, anticlockwise.

From Te Anau to Brod Bay, the Kepler starts out gently enough through a forest of red beech and mountain beech on the edge of Lake Te Anau, the largest lake in the South Island. Whether you wander in silence or converse with a companion, these first kilometres help to clear the mind of the recent hectic past and other unnecessary thoughts. The harder work begins with the climb up the east-facing hill from Brod Bay to the bushline through an entrancing forest covered in lichens. When you look closer into these masses of lichen they seem like complete universes in themselves. Darting between these mini-worlds are diminutive head-bopping and chirruping riflemen, along with bellbirds, tomtits, grey warblers and kākāriki. After almost an hour of steady climbing, the track arrives at a limestone rampart over 200 metres long and 60 metres high, which appears like a huge rippling wave frozen in the forest. This is a good place to catch your breath and contemplate the millions of years it took to form this incredible natural structure. Beyond here, the bushline opens onto tussock ridges, and the track leads to the over-built 50-bunk edifice of Luxmore Hut, high above Lake Te Anau. The expansive tops lie at an easy gradient, and all around are great stretches of water, mountains and sky.

During good weather it's worth heading down the side track close to Luxmore Hut to explore the nearby limestone cave.

OPPOSITE The South Fiord of Lake Te Anau and the Murchison Mountains from the Kepler Track SPENCER CLUBB

Brod Bay

Sloping into the hillside like an obliquely angled bullet hole, it remains about the same diameter, shape and ruler-straight gradient for at least several hundred metres, which was as far as I went with a fading torch. From the cave I wandered a short distance north across yellow–gold tussocks to look down onto the South Fiord of Lake Te Anau and up into the main reach of the lake itself. It was a view of enormous reach and grandeur. As the evening lengthened, long stretching bands of sunlight were lost to the forests, and the lake's shimmering waters became bathed in beautiful washes of hazy blues. That lakes appear in dreams as symbols of our vast unconsciousness is perhaps why they are so peaceful to our conscious mind— it's as though the act of gazing across water enables us to step

through a dark door in our heads and drown our worries in its larger undercurrents. Even smaller bodies of water hold surprises, as I discovered looking down onto tumbled ridges of beech forest amongst which numerous small kettle lakes, visible only from above, played point and counterpoint games with my mind's eye, causing the intervening ridges to pop up and down in optical riddles like an Escher artwork.

From Luxmore Hut, the next day's tramping is spent almost entirely above the bushline, winding around easily travelled

OPPOSITE Silver and mountain beech forest on the descent into the Iris Burn valley
OVERLEAF Morning light on the Murchison Mountains from near Luxmore Hut, with cloud filling the South Fiord of Lake Te Anau TOM BEESLEY

A frosted mosaic of speargrass on Mt Luxmore

mountain faces and ridges. The track zigzags a few times, then climbs gradually before commencing a long sidle under the northern faces of Mt Luxmore. The rocks around Mt Luxmore sparkle with crystals and mica, their grainy, gritty texture splashed in strong dark reds and blue–greys. They tend to break into large blocks, unlike the finer slates and shingles that characterise schist and greywacke mountains in the Southern Alps, and on certain outcrops form natural ruins like a stonemason's cast-offs. Many of these are 'plutonic' rocks that formed underground from molten rock but cooled extremely slowly, thereby forming very large crystals. The most unusual rocks are an ultramafic suite rich in magnesium and iron minerals. Dunite, an olive green rock found on the eastern slopes of Mt Luxmore, is one example. Indeed the Kepler Track, of all the walks described in this book, has the most interest for those with a geological bent. Here it's possible to point to the ground and roll your

tongue knowingly around such expressive words as gabbro, dunite, pegmatite, diorite and gneiss.

This second day, no matter what the weather (the well-marked track has two shelters—called Forest Burn and Hanging Valley—if the weather proves bad), will etch long-lasting images into your memory. When glancing down to place your feet you will see rocks and alpine tussocks, flowering herbs and mountain grasshoppers; when you look out you will see huge Fiordland vistas, and may even experience an almost vertiginous feeling of spaciousness. On a fine day the view south, west and north is across a sprawling sea of mountains that reach out to the horizon like wave upon wave of ocean swells. But if the weather is stormy, anxiety and awe will create a fine line between the exhilaration of being in such an exposed situation and your necessary concern to keep warm and on track.

Invariably, a full day on the tops leaves you thirsty, hungry and either hot or cold (I'm sure it's possible to feel both at once when you're tired), so when the track cuts steeply down into the comfort of the subalpine forest towards the Iris Burn Hut, you feel somewhat relieved to depart the tops. Shrubby groves of aromatic celery pines, or mountain toatoa, and bog and pygmy pines lead you into a lichen-encrusted mountain and silver beech forest. Further down, the understorey is composed of prickly swathes of shield fern, while orchards of mountain ribbonwood thrive on open slips. Vistas through the forest from creek crossings and slips give views into large sections of the broad, steep-sided Iris Burn valley.

From Iris Burn Hut, take a side track upstream for just 20 minutes, through a dense and mossy forest of ribbonwood and giant silver beech, to reach some falls on the Iris Burn. Here

OPPOSITE South Fiord of Lake Te Anau and the Murchison Mountains

the river tumbles over a bluff into a wide pool, next to which an enormous fallen trunk conveniently provides a place for an evening meditation in this beautiful spot.

By making an early start the following day you can walk all the way to Rainbow Reach carpark (allow seven to eight hours), or to the Te Anau outlet in 10–11 hours. But most prefer the five- or six-hour stroll down the Iris Burn to spend a third night at Moturau Hut on the shores of Lake Manapōuri. After the enormity of the elements and views of the previous day, it's a respite to walk in the enveloping warmth and security of tall beech forest—that is until about 45 minutes downstream, when an opening, named without poetry as 'the big slip of 1984', is reached after a short climb over a moraine hill where groves of ribbonwood and leathery-barked fuchsia trees create elfin interludes. The slide provides a sobering reminder that even the forest and its seeming security is just a graceful veneer over a turbulent landscape. During a period of exceptionally heavy rain in 1984, gravels and larger rocks from the obvious scar on the opposite hillside were strewn over the valley by a landslip. If you multiply this occurrence up and down the valley and then through every similar valley in Fiordland, in geological terms you'll perceive the inadequacy of post-Shakespearian clichés about this 'too too solid' earth. All nature is in flux, but with a timescale much longer than our lives, and so we witness only occasional glimpses of its continuing dynamism.

After the slip, you enter again the filtered green light of the beech forest, the walk being broken occasionally by smaller slips, stream fans and ferny gullies. Just as your pack begins to feel as heavy as it did on the first day, the track crosses the gravels of the Iris Burn's delta. With the hut only 45 minutes' tramp away, you can rest by Lake Manapōuri and look south across the water to the granite form of Mt Titiroa.

Beyond Moturau Hut, a boardwalk stretches out above a superb kettle bog, a soggy mire where tiny purple bladderworts, deep blue swamp orchids and diminutive sundews waver amongst rustling wires of rush and green sphagnum moss. Beyond the swamp's edges kahikatea, rimu and matai poke above the beech canopy, but in the stagnant water-laden soils of the mire these species grow only in stunted form. After several swamps are traversed, the trail reaches the Waiau River where, at the Rainbow Reach bridge, you can catch (in summer) a shuttle bus to Te Anau. Otherwise the track continues for a further three hours of forest and riverside walk to complete the circle back at the Lake Te Anau outlet.

OPPOSITE The foamy veil of the Iris Burn Falls cascades through beech forest close to Iris Burn Hut

Rona Island in Lake Manapōuri, from Moturau SHAUN BARNETT/BLACK ROBIN PHOTOGRAPHY
OPPOSITE Beech forest alongside the Iris Burn ROB BROWN

KEPLER TRACK

Fiordland National Park

DISTANCE 60 km

TIME REQUIRED 3–4 days

NEAREST TOWN Te Anau

BEST TIME TO WALK THE TRACK
October–April

FITNESS Moderate fitness required

The Kepler Track is constructed to a high
standard and has three huts with bunks,
mattresses and running water. Heating,
gas cooking facilities and flush toilets are
supplied between late October and April.
During this peak summer season, all huts
and campsites need to be booked well
in advance. At other times of the year,
trampers need to carry their own cooking
equipment. In winter through to late spring
the tops are snow-covered, and there
may be a risk of avalanches. Camping is
possible only at Brod Bay and at Iris Burn
Hut. Shuttle services are available from Te
Anau to and from the track, or else allow
about 45 minutes to walk to the track
start from Te Anau. Water taxis can also
be chartered to Brod Bay. Because this
route involves a day on the tops, good
equipment and knowledge of weather and
mountain navigation is required.

APPROXIMATE TRACK TIMES
(anticlockwise direction)
Control Gates to Brod Bay
5.5 km, 1.5 hours

Brod Bay to Mt Luxmore Hut
(50 bunks)
8.5 km, 3.5–4.5 hours

Mt Luxmore Hut to Iris Burn Hut
(54 bunks)
14.5 km, 5–6 hours

Iris Burn Hut to Moturau Hut
(40 bunks)
16 km, 5–6 hours

Moturau Hut to Rainbow Reach
6 km, 1.5–2 hours

Rainbow Reach to Control Gates
9.5 km, 2.5–3.5 hours

FURTHER INFORMATION
Fiordland National Park Visitor Centre
Lakefront Drive, PO Box 29,
Te Anau 9640
Tel: 03 249 /924
Email: fiordlandvc@doc.govt.nz

Book online at: www.doc.govt.nz
email: greatwalksbooking@doc.govt.nz
or tel: 0800 694 732

South Fiord

Lake Te Anau

shelter

shelter

Mt Luxmoore

limestone cave

Luxmoore Hut

Brod Bay

lls

Iris Burn Hut

TE ANAU

MOUNTAINS

control gates

START/END

Iris Burn

Moturau Hut

Rainbow Reach

Shallow Bay

carpark

Shallow Bay Hut

Lake Manapōuri

Waiau River

MILFORD TRACK

Fiordland is severe country with an uncompromising climate, which makes the Milford Track all the more remarkable for the relative ease with which it conveys people into the heart of this rugged wilderness. Not that walking the Milford Track is an effortless undertaking—it's more that the Milford's well-constructed path belies Fiordland's severity as it comfortably steers trampers along two immense glaciated valleys and over a high pass within a spectacular landscape of mountains, snow-fields and deep-green forests. In effect, walkers of the Milford are granted all the rewards of tramping in this exceptional mountain area, yet spared the struggles necessary to tramp in most other Fiordland valleys.

What many aren't spared walking the Milford is wet weather. It rains frequently (on average 7–10 metres a year) and torrentially, rapidly transforming the landscape as waterfalls formed in an instant career down previously blank rock faces, gentle watercourses become seething torrents, and water flows across the valleys—taking everything in its path like the mythical Assyrian army. Water is thus a dominant motif on the Milford, although not one that should deter you because the experience of a Fiordland storm—seen from the safety of a bridge—can be just as exhilarating as the stupendous vistas of a fine day. Beyond the immediate and awe-inspiring effects of a Fiordland inundation, water also works in more subtle ways, sustaining the luxuriant coatings of moss and epiphytes in its forests, and

filling the pools, cascades and waterfalls that have added so much character to the Clinton and Arthur valleys. Gigantic Ice Age glaciers of frozen water carved the walls of these two valleys, and even today frozen snow released in mammoth winter avalanches continues to alter the landscape and vegetation. That water forms a major theme on the Milford Track is dramatically confirmed by the 580-metre Sutherland Falls, among New Zealand's highest waterfalls (its status as the highest waterfall was only recently eclipsed by discovery of a higher one, also in Fiordland) and also by the fact that—uniquely for this country—reaching the track requires passage across two large bodies of water—Lake Te Anau and Milford Sound.

During the Milford's 'season' (between late October and mid-April) the track is always walked over four days from Lake Te Anau to Milford Sound. Along with the logistics of simply getting to this distant corner of the country, huts must be booked and transport to and from the track arranged well in advance—often months ahead of your trip. But from Glade Wharf on Lake Te Anau, all that passes into memory as you wander easily up the lower Clinton Valley alongside the clear, deep pools of the Clinton River. Inside this quintessential South Island forest of moss-draped red and silver beech, robins

OPPOSITE Swingbridge crossing the Clinton River at the start of the Milford Track LUIS SAN MIGUEL

Beech forest overhangs peaceful pools in the Clinton River's north branch, upstream of Clinton Forks

and tomtits make delicate appearances and the whole valley is alerted to your presence by the strange calls of paradise ducks and the noisy wing-thumping departures of startled wood pigeons. Moving at an easy pace, it takes about two hours to reach Clinton Forks where the river branches west and north, and the mountains rise in deep blue complement to the pale sky and the shining green forest foliage.

The forks is a good place to stop to pay homage to the creators of this 120-year-old track—Quintin Mackinnon and Donald Sutherland. In 1888 Mackinnon and Sutherland were commissioned to cut a trail linking Lake Te Anau to Milford

Sound, which at that time could only be reached by sea. With Sutherland working from the Arthur Valley, Mackinnon, accompanied by Ernest Mitchell, set off up the Clinton and worked for three weeks in virtually unremitting rain and misery before crossing the pass, later named after him, on 17 October 1888. At a river beach in the Arthur Valley they cooked and ate a blue duck, not in celebration but to assuage a gnawing hunger. Then, after stumbling onto the track cut by Sutherland as far as Sutherland Falls, they made their way

OPPOSITE The path up the Clinton Valley

38

to Milford Sound. Mackinnon returned over the pass a few days later, once again in appalling weather. Unbowed by the experience, he remained in the area and established himself as the track's first guide until his untimely drowning in Lake Te Anau in 1892. Sutherland lived in Milford Sound where his wife Elizabeth ran an accommodation house for the increasing number of tourists participating in the fashionably new recreations of forest and mountain walking. It's difficult to know if either man quite realised how favoured their route would become, but its future popularity was assured in 1908 when photographs and articles appeared in the *London Spectator* boldly proclaiming the Milford Track as 'the finest walk in the world'.

Clinton Hut is the first night's shelter for independent walkers. The immensity of the Fiordland landscape is truly felt beyond the hut on the second afternoon's walk to Mintaro Hut in the upper reaches of the Clinton River West Branch. After the tranquility of the lower Clinton, the landscape has an austere beauty, accentuated when the harsher afternoon light plays on huge scarred faces of rock. Further on, the dark trees of the 'black forest' (a pure stand of tall and twisted silver beech) presage a landscape desolated time and again by landslips and avalanches. Ducks quack from among drowned trees in a lake formed by a rockfall, while adventurous colonising plants such as wineberry, mountain ribbonwood, flax, toetoe and the prickly mountain holly spread out across the scenes of devastation. Despite this new growth, the long shadow of next winter's avalanches hangs over any confident assertions of life.

With the prospects of the climb up to Mackinnon Pass in the morning, the night spent at Mintaro may well have an element of wakeful self-doubt, in contrast to the confident hoots of moreporks and occasional screeching of weka, or even kiwi. All things pass however, and having roused yourself for the day ahead you are quickly lifted into another world where groves of ribbonwood spray white petals across the lower track, and stunted beech trees are draped in more moss, it would seem, than their own mass. Zigzagging easily up under the near vertical bluffs of Mt Balloon, the track climbs into herbfields containing the ubiquitous Mount Cook buttercup to reach the 1069-metre pass. Marking the summit is a surreal concrete and rock cairn emblazoned with the strange notation that it was put there in remembrance of Mackinnon by none other than the Gaelic Society and the Otago Rugby Union (Mackinnon was an outstanding rugby player), with the help of the New Zealand government. If the day is clear, a 15-minute walk towards Mt Balloon takes you away from your fellow walkers, though sadly never far enough away from the alienating buzz of planes and helicopters. Below lies the tarn-spotted pass, and beyond is Mt Hart, its ridges carving and splitting into monstrous mountain cul-de-sacs. To the right, under the precariously sloped ice shelf of the Jervois Glacier, a series of waterfalls pour down Mt Elliot's fluted rock face.

For some, the long descent off the pass into the Arthur Valley brings a painful awareness of knees and ankles, and a reminder that the ascent of any high pass or mountain is just half the journey. Ultimately however, the track crosses Roaring Burn to reach Quintin Lodge. After a rest, and despite the anguish in your legs, the two-kilometre side trip to Sutherland Falls is obligatory because not only are the falls truly awe-inspiring, but even the track's tunnel of glowing red–gold fuchsia, dark green prickly shield ferns, beech trees and tree ferns are enough to compel you forward. As you stand beneath the mesmeric leaps of water, picture William Quill, who in 1890 climbed the sheer wall immediately beside these falls and at the top discovered the lake that now bears his name.

OPPOSITE Moss-covered boulder in the Clinton River ROB BROWN

Sutherland Falls plunges 580 metres from Lake Quill

beauty, the track crosses numerous areas wrecked by landslides and rockfalls. Though these eerie scenes reek of dead plants and shattered rocks, rockfalls are a necessary part of the natural cycle in Fiordland's valleys, for they restore minerals to soils leached by the vast amount of rain that falls here every year. About a thousand years ago a huge rockfall dammed the lower Arthur River and formed Lake Ada. When the lake level is low, tree stumps protrude through the water's surface, a collection of decaying sentinels speaking silently of an earlier time.

With a boat to catch from Sandfly Point on the last afternoon, and an awareness that this was the last day of a great trip, my mind wandered more frequently than usual. It occurred to me that the Milford Track itself is a path of history through the natural world. Although it is a restrained imprint, rocks nonetheless have been laboriously shifted, boardwalks built over swamps, rivers bridged and a sloping stairway dynamited out of solid rock around Lake Ada. It is nice to think that for over a hundred years now people have walked this track, enriching their imaginations and singing the praises of this precious protected landscape. The climax of the track at Milford Sound is fittingly Wagnerian in scale, with steeply angled rock faces rising sheer for thousands of metres from the dark depths of the sound. Engulfed by this scene, it is hard not to feel privileged being able to spend time journeying on tracks such as the Milford.

Beyond Quintin Lodge, the track skirts the Arthur River, at one point offering a last backward glance at Sutherland Falls, before continuing to reach Dumpling Hut. The final day in the Arthur Valley leads down the line of Sutherland's old track to Milford Sound, and soon reaches one of the most picturesque spots on the Milford Track—Bell Rock. From here you look into Mackay Falls, a scene that is resplendent with power and grace in heavy rain. In contrast to this more conventional

OPPOSITE Early morning light on Mt Elliot and Mackinnon Pass ROB SUISTED/NATURESPIC.COM
OVERLEAF The memorial cairn to Quintin Mackinnon on Mackinnon Pass GRAHAM DAINTY

Thick moss draping subalpine beech forest is evidence of Fiordland's high rainfall
OPPOSITE Surrounded by ferns and beech forest, Mackay Creek emerges on the Milford Track at a bouldery cascade known as Mackay Falls
OVERLEAF Mitre Peak, and the prominent rounded shoulder of The Lion to the right, in Milford Sound

MILFORD TRACK
Fiordland National Park

DISTANCE 54 km

TIME REQUIRED 4 days

NEAREST CENTRE Te Anau

BEST TIME TO WALK THE TRACK November–April

FITNESS Moderate fitness required

The Milford Track is constructed to a high standard. However, the weather can be severe and good equipment is essential. Snow can fall on Mackinnon Pass at any time of the year, and torrential rain can make sections of the track impassable. All huts are supplied with gas cookers, mattresses and heating. Huts must be booked in advance between late October and April and, given the popularity of this track, early booking is advised. During the 'season', the track is always walked from Lake Te Anau to Milford Sound. Outside this period booking is not required, though gas facilities are removed from the huts, and at times huts are closed for maintenance. Some bridges are also removed from the path of winter avalanches. Trampers should be aware of the high avalanche risk in this area during winter and spring. There are a number of ways to reach the track from Te Anau, including float plane, kayak and water taxi, and similar arrangements can be made at the Milford Sound end for the return journey to Te Anau. Guided walks are also available on the Milford using private lodges.

APPROXIMATE TRACK TIMES

Glade Wharf to Clinton Hut (40 bunks)
5 km, 1–1.5 hours

Clinton Hut to Mintaro Hut (40 bunks)
16.5 km, 6 hours

Mintaro Hut to Dumpling Hut (40 bunks)
14 km, 6–7 hours

Dumpling Hut to Sandfly Point (40 bunks)
18 km, 5–7 hours

FURTHER INFORMATION

Fiordland National Park Visitor Centre
Lakefront Drive, PO Box 29,
Te Anau 9640
Tel: 03 249 7924
Email: fiordlandvc@doc.govt.nz

Book online at: www.doc.govt.nz
email: greatwalksbooking@doc.govt.nz
or tel: 0800 694 732

MILFORD SOUND

Sandfly Point
END

Lake Ada

Arthur River

Bell Rock
Mackay Falls

Dumpling Hut

Jervois
Glacier

Mt Elliot

Quintin
Lodge

Mt Balloon

Sutherland
Falls

shelter

Lake
Quill

Mackinnon Pass

Mt Hart

Mintaro Hut

Pompalona Lodge

Clinton
Forks

Clinton River

Clinton Hut

Eglinton River

Glade House

wharf
START

Lake
Te Anau

SH94 to TE ANAU

N

ROUTEBURN TRACK

The Routeburn Track is a high mountain traverse of the Ailsa and Humboldt mountains, two spectacular glacier-sculpted sandstone ranges wedged between the granite peaks of Fiordland's Darran Mountains and the crumbling schist ranges of Mount Aspiring National Park. If you start the Routeburn from its southern end and climb to the grand viewpoint of Key Summit, you almost immediately gain an impression of the impact that glaciers had on the southern South Island landscape—in fact everywhere you look is a postscript to the last Ice Age that peaked 15,000 to 20,000 years ago. Below, the Hollyford Valley describes the classic U-shape of a glacier-carved valley, and its steep sides retain the classical imprints of a post-glacial landscape: hanging valleys, headwalls, cirque basins and aquamarine tarns. Across the valley, where remnant glaciers persist on the highest Darran summits, are fine glacier-honed 'arete peaks' like Pyramid and Christina, while northwards lies the beautifully rendered Emily Peak above Lake Mackenzie in the Ailsa Mountains. If morning cloud has filled the Hollyford to the bushline you can imagine that cloud as a huge glacier, fed by numerous side glaciers, and so start to comprehend the enormous drama that took place here when the ice was on the move. Indeed, the glacier that filled the Hollyford was so deep that it flowed over Key Summit (today a forest-fringed mountain bogland) and dispersed tongues of ice into the Eglinton and Greenstone valleys, while the main flow continued down the Hollyford to well beyond the present shore at Martins Bay. The glacial imprint appears so fresh because the granites and sandstones of these dramatic mountains are more resistant to the weathering forces that elsewhere have worn away the glacial record. At any time of year, even in midsummer, walking the Routeburn can become a meditation on the language of glaciers as you move beneath sculpted faces and ridges, past Lakes Howden, Mackenzie and Harris—created when the ice retreated—and past large boulders sure to be heavily scratched and serrated by broken rocks dragged over their surfaces while embedded in ice.

The Routeburn is most often walked in three days (with evenly spaced stops at Lake Mackenzie and Routeburn Falls), but make sure you allow sufficient time at Lake Mackenzie to explore the montane forest on its shores and the alpine areas beyond.

From the Milford Road, and after the Key Summit turn-off, the way to Lake Mackenzie Hut continues past Lake Howden through mountain and silver beech forests, and the occasional open frosty area laid bare by avalanches and floods now graced with shield ferns and deciduous ribbonwood (the latter identifiable by its light-green foliage and white hibiscus-like flowers).

OPPOSITE Lake Mackenzie lies in a glaciated basin in the Ailsa Mountains ROB BROWN

In such places, even in summer, the sun seldom touches their blue shade and the creek water is so cold and fresh to drink that it sears your head. Earland Falls, a picturesque cascade 90 minutes from Lake Howden, is a delightful place to doff packs on a hot afternoon and relax among the sun-warmed boulders and pools below the falls.

During my evening at Lake Mackenzie, I found myself inside an archaic, chaotic and quite beautiful mountain beech forest on the lake's southern shore. I find it hard to write about the kind of visual pleasure such places impress upon me (and there are many of them in the Southern Alps) because sensual impulses are not so easily rendered in words, and because I'm never sure if it's the pull of the place or my mood at the time that initiates the excitement. Squat, tough and bent trees, drenched in mosses and lichens, reached their roots over moss-covered glacial boulders into deeper realms of moss on the soggy forest floor. Nearby, water lapped against discordant piles of rocks, and Emily Peak and other mountains rose above the shadowed valley, glowing eerily in the evening light and standing over me, mute and muscular. I spent the next morning engrossed by the forest, lake and mountain faces, wandering slowly and musing about all kinds of things—as you do when you're entranced by a world not of your making.

Beyond Lake Mackenzie, you tramp up a zigzag path, leading to the Hollyford face. All of the day along the face to Harris Saddle and beyond to Routeburn Falls—about a 15-kilometre walk—is spent in the alpine zone exposed to the elements, which must be in your favour before you start. Clear or even intermittently clear weather to Harris Saddle allows panoramas of the Darran Mountains, the highest of which are the blocky ramparts of Tutoko (2723 metres) and Madeline (2536 metres). As you walk, alpine grasshoppers jump away from your feet in random spring-loaded leaps, and alpine tussocks and

flowers unique to New Zealand waver in the constant breezes that blow across the Hollyford face.

In the high summer, flowers crowd these wide slopes, and when admiring their beauty it's also worth pondering the fact that about 90 per cent of New Zealand's mountain plants aren't found anywhere else in the world. That's because for the last 85 million years New Zealand has been geographically isolated from any other land, allowing its cargo of plants to adapt and specialise. While it seems surprising that plants survive at all in high altitudes, they have done so by evolving ways to cope with the impoverished soils and harsh alpine environment found throughout New Zealand's mountain areas. Most of our native alpine plants grow between the treeline and rocky screes: tussocks and sprawling shrubby plants are found in a narrow band above the treeline and higher still grow the flowering herbs, tall and short snow tussocks, many species of sharp speargrasses, cushion plants and alpine grasses. Of the herbs, the most revered are the white-flowered, glossy-leaved Mount Cook buttercup (the largest buttercup in the world) and closely related yellow buttercups. But much more numerous than the buttercups are mountain daisies from the *Celmisia* family of plants, though foxgloves and gentians are also common, and the South Island edelweiss, recognised by its white woolly flowerhead and fuzzy silver leaves, will be found on higher outcrops. Boggy places like those on Key Summit and in the Harris basin are another feature of the alpine zone. In these grow a variety of moisture-loving plants—sphagnum mosses, sundews, bladderworts, bog pines, daisies, orchids, the white caltha and the bronze forget-me-not. Tread carefully, though preferably not at all, among these fragile, easily damaged boglands.

Evening light at Lake Mackenzie SHAUN BARNETT/BLACK ROBIN PHOTOGRAPHY
OPPOSITE Boulders from the landslide that dammed Lake Mackenzie lie near the lake's subterranean outlet

The Darran Mountains and Hollyford Valley from Conical Hill PETR HLAVACEK

The sidle along the Hollyford face continues for about two hours before turning sharply up to Harris Saddle/Tarahaka Whakatipu (1255 metres) where there are two shelters—one for independent trampers, and the other a private one for guided walkers. If conditions are fine it's worth climbing the 250 metres up to Conical Hill for views of extraordinary spaciousness. Eastwards, across linear glacier-smoothed slabs of tussock and rock, lie Lake Harris and the amphitheatre of scattered boulders known as the Valley of the Trolls; behind the lake a squat Mt Xenicus (an outlier of the Humboldt Mountains), the Harris basin and, way beyond, the Dart Valley are visible. To the south and west a visual line leads off the summits of Tutoko and Madeline deep into the Hollyford Valley, the broad reaches of Lake McKerrow and the shimmering silver of the Tasman Sea.

There are few experiences more elating and relaxing than to reach a high pass with plenty of time left to get to your next destination. Having reached Harris Saddle, the remaining journey is an easy downhill walk past Lake Harris and the rough tussock meadows of the Harris basin. If you have the time and weather to dawdle these last kilometres, twilight is a wonderful time to stroll into Routeburn Falls Hut, which is set among dwarf beech trees near a dancing watercourse and the Routeburn Falls. The eastward facing hut is not a place to leave too early in the morning either. Rather, get up early, make a cup of tea, sit down on the veranda and let the sun rise over the ranges beyond the Dart River to warm your tired body and lazy soul. Then share vicariously in the energy and stubborn inquisitiveness of the local kea on their customary morning visit.

OPPOSITE A tramper looking west to the Darran Mountains PETR HLAVACEK
OVERLEAF Looking down onto the Routeburn Flats PETR HLAVACEK

Rest assured, the last day of the journey continues in the easy downward pace that began after lunch the day before, although the track passes largely through a blanketing beech forest in contrast to the previous day's more raw exposure to the elements. However you soon discover, when crossing a large landslide, that all is not as eternally comforting as it seems. The slip is reached not long after tall forest gains an encompassing grip on the land above Routeburn Flat. In 1994, after several days of torrential rain, the scant soils on this slope gave way and thundered toward the flat, releasing a huge quantum of energy and debris. Despite the immediate catastrophic impacts of landslides, beech forests thrive on such crises; even after a minor event such as the fall of a single tree, the extra light falling through the canopy triggers strong and rapid growth in beech seedlings, which often wait years for just that chance. And as can be seen around the valley where variations in the heights of trees indicate the sites of past slips and rockfalls, beech forests have coped with crises for thousands of years. Beyond the slip, order returns, and on a sunny day the views and containment of the tussock-covered flats, where the west and north branches of the Route Burn meet, take on a prelapsarian warmth with, ironically, the only raucous discord likely to come from pairs of paradise ducks asserting their territorial demands. Back in the forest, tomtits and bush robins approach with Eden-like innocence, though more than likely they are interested in snapping up any insects stirred by your footfall through the leaf litter.

'The sump'—a bottleneck of tree trunks and boulders thrust haphazardly together as if a giant had crushed his marbles among his pick-up sticks—is encountered where the track enters the top of the forested Route Burn gorge. Called 'the sump' because the river disappears into this morass, it is a place of dread and awe, yet exhilarating to stand beside, knowing that the track can be regained a mere 30 metres above. In this shadowed valley, dead trees lie stripped of their bark and jammed at awkward angles, their skeletal forms shining blue, grey and cream. Somewhere around here in 1864 three prospectors, Alphonse 'George' Barrington and his companions James Farrell and Antoine Simonin struggled back towards Lake Wakatipu after an epic journey of four months in the West Coast valleys of the Hollyford, Pyke and Cascade, and the lifeless Red Hills region. Living on a woefully inadequate diet of occasional kākāpo, weka, robins and the like, and badly frostbitten, Barrington wrote, not without the spirit of irony and strong will that kept him going: 'If fasting and praying is of any value to sinners, we ought soon to become saints.' Stare into the sump, contemplate their agony and smile wryly at Barrington's indomitable wit.

In counterpoint to the gorge and the sump are the welcoming red beech trees in the last hour before the road end. Such groves create a world of green I shall never tire of, neither forbidding nor over-bright, their layered leaves an aesthetic repose after the immensity of the vistas of the last few days.

OPPOSITE Routeburn Flats and the Humboldt Mountains at sunset PETR HLAVACEK OVERLEAF Tall red beech forest in the last kilometres to Routeburn Shelter

ROUTEBURN TRACK

Fiordland and Mount Aspiring national parks

DISTANCE 32 km

TIME REQUIRED 2–3 days

NEAREST CENTRES Glenorchy and Te Anau

BEST TIME TO WALK THE TRACK October–April

FITNESS Moderate fitness required

The Routeburn Track traverses parts of both Fiordland and Mount Aspiring national parks. The mountainous terrain and exposure to bad weather require good equipment. There are four huts, all supplied with gas cookers, mattresses and heating. Camping is permitted next to Mackenzie and Routeburn Flats huts, as well as at Greenstone Saddle. Between late October and April, hut accommodation and campsites have to be booked well in advance. Outside this period gas facilities are removed from the huts and your own cooking equipment is required. In winter the track is snow-covered with risks from avalanches, particularly on the Hollyford face. The track can be walked in either direction. Guided walks are also available on the Routeburn using private lodges. Regular transport services operate to and from the track.

APPROXIMATE TRACK TIMES
(Milford Road to Routeburn Shelter):

The Divide to Lake Howden Hut (28 bunks)
3.4 km, 1–1.5 hours

Lake Howden Hut to Lake Mackenzie Hut
(50 bunks)
8.6 km, 3–4 hours

Lake Mackenzie Hut to Routeburn Falls Hut
(48 bunks)
11.3 km, 5–6 hours

Routeburn Falls Hut to Routeburn Flats Hut
(20 bunks)
2.3 km, 1–1.5 hours

Routeburn Flats to Routeburn Shelter
6.5 km, 2–3 hours

FURTHER INFORMATION
Queenstown/Whakatipu-wai-Māori
Visitor Centre
50 Stanley Street, PO Box 811
Queenstown 9300
Tel: 03 442 7935
Email: queenstownvc@doc.govt.nz

Book online at www.doc.govt.nz
email: greatwalksbooking@doc.govt.nz
or tel: 0800 694 732

DARRAN MOUNTAINS

SH94 to
MILFORD SOUND

The Divide Shelter
START

N

SH94 to
TE ANAU

Valley of the Trolls

Mt Xenicus

Conical Hill

Harris Basin

Lake Harris

Harris Saddle

shelter

Routeburn Falls Hut

Routeburn Flats Hut

'The sump'

END

Route Burn

Routeburn Shelter

Routeburn Falls

Emily Peak

Lake Mackenzie

AILSA MOUNTAINS

HUMBOLDT MOUNTAINS

Lake Mackenzie Hut

Dart River

to GLENORCHY

Earland Falls

Howden Hut

Lake Howden

HEAPHY TRACK

Two contrasting landscapes are likely to linger in your mind after you've walked the Heaphy: one, a high, silent, tussock plateau; the other, a loud coastline where waves reach brashly towards groves of tropical palms and flowering rātā. These contrasts often accentuate divergent emotions of fear and attraction, awe and intimacy—it is all part of the appealing variety you experience on this traverse through forests and ancient geological structures in the northwest of Kahurangi National Park.

Most begin the Heaphy Track from Brown Hut at the eastern end of the trail in Golden Bay, and allow between three and five days to reach its conclusion on the West Coast. Setting out from here delegates all the climbing to the first day, leaving the easy wander along the western beaches, with considerably lightened packs, until last. Once beyond the first paddocks and scrubby spurs, the track enters a diverse forest that includes huge old red and hard beeches, rimu and miro, with distinctive mikimiki and toro trees in the understorey. As the zigzag climb continues, the intimacy of the forest is broken by occasional supplejack tangles and large landslides. The benched track follows an easy grade up the hillside along a route constructed in 1893 to allow packhorses passage through the area. Thanks to those who built the track, you can—for the first hours at least—let your mind wander freely, or disengage completely, without worrying too much about where to put your feet, though you will be pulled back in lyrical moments by attentive fantails

and tomtits or the distinctive calls of kākā, bellbird and tūī. The track crosses streams at regular intervals, and windows in the forest open towards the granite summits of the Lead Hills and Mt Olympus across the Aorere Valley, and beyond to the Dragons Teeth on the Douglas Range. Major lookouts occur at the Aorere Shelter, 11 kilometres from Brown River, where mountain cabbage trees protrude disjunctively, and a further three kilometres on at Flanagans Corner. The latter, the highest point on the track, offers a first westward glance to Perry Saddle Hut, about 30 minutes away.

It's worth starting early the next day before the sun banishes the moody blue cast and low mists that often lie across the Gouland Downs, about an hour's descent from Perry Saddle. The downs immediately make an impression by their strangeness: the high rolling plateau of open tussock and occasional forest contrasts with the rustling patches of mountain neinei and silver beech. Perhaps the downs landscape catches you off guard because mountainous country isn't meant to be so smooth and flattish, and forests aren't supposed to sit above alpine tussocklands. For whatever reason, it's queer country and nearly everyone feels something of its eeriness, even if only retrospectively, once down in the semi-tropical forests

OPPOSITE Weathered granite outcrop on Scotts Beach ROB BROWN

of the Heaphy Valley. For those with a mind for geology, the Gouland Downs, one of the oldest landforms in New Zealand, is fascinating terrain. Like the Mt Arthur Tablelands to the east and the Matiri plateaux in the south, the downs are what remain of a huge low-lying peneplain that was formed 80 to 100 million years ago out of 400- to 500-million-year old siltstones and sandstones. This vast peneplain eventually sank below the sea, to be overlaid by limestone, before the land was raised again in the present phase of mountain building. Much of the limestone has been eroded off, revealing the old surface again which now stands over 600 metres above sea level. Next to tussocks and light-grey skeletons of dwarfed mānuka on the track's edge, tiny purple orchids protrude from the mud and gravels. With the notable exception of its fertile islands of limestone, the downs' soils have been severely leached of nutrients. Consequently few plants other than the tussocks, alpine shrubs and flowers that have adapted to these conditions grow with any vigour in this country. There are many rare plants here and some, like the foxglove *Ourisia goulandiana*, as its name suggests, grow only on these downs.

Specialisations such as this, and the rarity of many plants here and elsewhere in Kahurangi influenced the course of events that led to this vast region of northwest Nelson being declared New Zealand's thirteenth national park in 1996. Geological variety and the presence of the country's oldest landforms were other factors, along with the significance of the area for native wildlife. This western region of the park, and Gouland Downs in particular, remains a stronghold for the endangered great spotted kiwi, and while you would have to be determined to sight one of these large nocturnal creatures in the wild, you will quite likely hear their screeching calls after dark. By day the flightless western weka and spirited flocks of pipits will be the most common birds seen, and if you're very lucky, you might glimpse the diminutive fernbird whose cryptic colours allow it to merge into the rushes and tussocks.

Two hours from Perry Saddle is the old Gouland Downs Hut, with the newer Saxon Hut another two hours farther on. Both are good bases for exploring the limestone karst (karst is a Czech term for water-worn) landscape, and also the plants of the area, which reach their flowering best during midsummer. As you move over the downs the track traverses tussock flats where rivers like the Big cut raw into the old peneplain and begin coiling and curling in slow meanders before their sudden descent into mossy beech forest. Near the confluence of the Saxon River and Blue Duck Creek, the geology abruptly changes. Now, on the way up to the Mackay Downs and towards Mackay Hut, the ancient sedimentary rocks of the peneplain are replaced by coarse granite that provides the rest of the track's stolid bedrock (with the exception of the dramatic limestone landscapes of the lower Heaphy Valley and Kōhaihai Bluff). Mackay Downs does not provide vistas as expansive as those of the Gouland. Instead the track weaves through a maze of tussock- and scrub-covered basins enclosed by forested hills on the side of Mt Teddy. Large yellowy-grey granite 'core stones' rise above stunted rātā, *Dracophyllum*, mountain toatoa and mānuka. Eventually Mackay Hut looms on a knoll above the track and the intimacy of this country relents, satisfying a desire for wider horizons and giving a wonderful view down to the Tasman Sea just beyond the mouth of the Heaphy River.

At Mackay Hut, the Heaphy Track leaves the rolling downs landscape and begins its long, gradual descent into the forests along the Heaphy River and towards the sea. In terms of the altitude surrendered, the evenness of the gradient, the un-

OPPOSITE The upper reaches of the Saxon River on Gouland Downs PETR HLAVACEK

70

Tussock grasses in afternoon sun at Gouland Downs Hut PETR HLAVACEK
OPPOSITE Stunted alpine vegetation grows among rocky outcrops on the Gouland Downs

Subalpine tussock grasslands on the Gouland Downs, looking east towards the Gouland Range

broken mantle of deep-green forest and the hypnotic effects of the track's gentle and endlessly repeating curves, the route between Mackay and Lewis huts is not dissimilar to the first day. However there are some differences. In the wetter western forests, mosses and ferns are far more common, and rimu and rātā grow more abundantly as can be expected on the West Coast. By the time you reach Lewis Hut, the stark austerity of the downs has been washed into memory by the luxuriance of the enveloping forest, and coastal/tropical associations are blatantly manifest in the dense tangles of epiphytes and lianes, along with the appearance of the first scattered nīkau palms.

If tramping is a process by which sweat and toil is the price paid for entering realms where the soul is uplifted by wild nature, then (for those heading westwards) Lewis Hut marks the trade-off point between effort and reward. From here to Kōhaihai the track rarely climbs more than a few metres above river level or the high-tide line, and the scenery is always superb. Heading downriver, the track wends between exquisite avenues of nīkau palms and tree ferns, and massive northern rātā clear the surrounding canopy, festooned in perching and climbing plants. Kiekie and supplejack vines make much of this forest quite impenetrable, and warmth-loving species like kawakawa, rangiora and kōwhai complement the forest's exotic nature.

OPPOSITE Beech trees, kiekie vines and tree ferns proliferate in the lush Heaphy forest

Nīkau palms sprout clusters of flowers from
the base of the lowest branch

Further enhancing this section along the river's final meander to the coast is a dramatic array of limestone landforms, including a rank of bluffs that not only walls in the southern bank, but also provides intriguing track-side architecture.

Where rivers meet the sea are often places of physical and psychic power, though few carry the consistent intensity of the Heaphy River mouth just below Heaphy Hut. A large surf invariably runs hard into the river, as it rushes across the swollen face of the sand. After three or four days walking, the almost violent power of the place seems paradoxically to create a sense of inner peace and contentment, especially at dusk when the sun boils into the western sea behind the rising spray of breaking waves. The river mouth area—the site of a Māori settlement and seasonal camp dating to 1380 AD—is sacred to Ngāi Tahu and, consequently, was excluded from

the national park. It is one of the few sites in the whole of the northwest South Island occupied by humans for any extended time, and the discovery of stone flints here suggests there was once a thriving trade in stone tools made at the camp from greenstone, argillite, chert and obsidian imported from other parts of the country.

It won't matter much what the weather does on the last day from Heaphy Hut to Kōhaihai Shelter because this is a wonderful walk in any conditions. When it's wild and stormy, the beaches are covered with pulsing, creamy foam and the sea thunders landwards from the horizon in huge sets of waves, though you can always find quiet respite from the rain and wind among groves of nīkau palms. Conversely, when it's sunny and hot and the swell's not too huge the ambience is more that of a tropical island. The five-hour walk to the road end across headlands and beaches can be strung out over a whole day in the knowledge that all the streams are bridged and the only major climb is the short ascent over the saddle between Scotts Beach and Kōhaihai Shelter, leaving you time to savour the golden sands, subtropical forest and the unceasing pounding of the surf.

OPPOSITE Nīkau palms growing on the
Heaphy coast ANDRIS APSE
OVERLEAF Boulder beach and nīkau forest at sunset on the
Heaphy coast ROB BROWN

HEAPHY TRACK
Kahurangi National Park

DISTANCE 82 km

TIME REQUIRED 4–6 days

NEAREST CENTRES Collingwood (Golden Bay); Karamea (West Coast)

BEST TIME TO WALK THE TRACK November–April

FITNESS Moderate fitness required

The Heaphy Track is constructed to a high standard and has seven huts including Brown Hut at the Aorere Valley road end. Huts must be booked all year round. All huts except Gouland Downs Hut have gas cookers, mattresses and heating. Designated campsites exist near all seven huts, as well as at Aorere Shelter, Katipo Shelter, Scotts Beach and Kōhaihai. A number of shuttles and buses service both ends of the track during the summer. Light aircraft can be chartered to enable a return to vehicles at either end of the track. Trampers should be aware that mountain bikers are allowed on the track between 1 May and 30 September.

APPROXIMATE TRACK TIMES
(from Aorere Valley, Golden Bay):

Brown Hut (16 bunks) to Perry Saddle Hut (28 bunks)
17.5 km, 5–6 hours

Perry Saddle Hut to Gouland Downs Hut (8 bunks)
7 km, 2 hours

Gouland Downs Hut to Saxon Hut (16 bunks)
5.4 km, 1.5 hours

Saxon Hut to James Mackay Hut (28 bunks)
11.8 km, 3 hours

James Mackay Hut to Lewis Hut (20 bunks)
12.5 km, 3.5–4 hours

Lewis Hut to Heaphy Hut (32 bunks)
8 km, 2.5–3 hours

Heaphy Hut to Kōhaihai Shelter
16.2 km, 5–6 hours

FURTHER INFORMATION
Golden Bay Area Office
Department of Conservation
62 Commercial Street, PO Box 166
Takaka 7142
Tel: 03 525 8026
Email: goldenbayao@doc.govt.nz

Karamea Information and Resource Centre
Main Road, Karamea 7893
Tel: 03 782 6652
Email: info@karameainfo.co.nz
Website: www.karameainfo.co.nz

Book online at www.doc.govt.nz
email: greatwalksbooking@doc.govt.nz
or tel: 0800 694 732

Tasman Sea

Heaphy Hut

GUNNER DOWNS

Lewis Hut

Lewis River

Heaphy River

Mackay Hut

MACKAY DOWNS

Mt Teddy

Blue Duck Ck

Saxon River

Saxon Hut

GOULAND DOWNS

Gouland Downs Hut

Spey River

Big River

Perry Saddle Hut

Flanagan's Corner

shelter

Brown Hut

START

Aorere River

to COLLINGWOOD

ABEL TASMAN COAST TRACK

Whether you walk north or south along the Abel Tasman National Park Coast Track makes little difference to your encounter with this quiet coast. Within a few hours, whichever direction you walk, are repeating themes of water, sand, rock and forest, and enchanting sequences of small sheltered beaches and shallow tidal inlets. In many ways the Coast Track is the hardest to write about, yet the easiest to enjoy. It's difficult to be overly expressive or adjectival because the forest isn't continuously great (in fact there are considerable areas of gorse and low scrub), the track itself is so easy and repetitive (where's the challenge?), the geology consists of granite, granite and more granite, and even the beauty of the beaches is plainly self-evident. Merely being on the sand induces a pleasing soporific effect—the body and mind doodle along like the track itself, stopping frequently in blank seas of blue and gold.

The point is almost reached where the coast's picturesque qualities, easy access, comfortable facilities and the degenerate state of the forest blinds you to the exceptional impact that some particular features have. Sculpted granite headlands, green beech leaves against jet black tree trunks, koru fern forms, and sunrise golds on sand ripples and akeake trunks—all have lifted me to a high state of delight, suggesting that the Coast Track's greatest impact is not in its overall qualities, but in its details.

Undoubtedly the Abel Tasman Coast Track is the most popular multi-day track in New Zealand because of its ease (in summer you can do it in sandshoes or sandals) and its swimmable sandy beaches, fringed in places by lush vegetation and ferns that evoke a semi-tropical mood. The track can be walked at any time of the year, though don't let its tropical appearance fool you; in winter it gets cold at night and only the hardiest swim.

Access, too, is much easier than for most other New Zealand walks, with daily bus services from Nelson to Mārahau, Tōtaranui and Wainui, and water taxis that call at many locations along the coast. Four large huts, well situated beside the ocean, are conveniently spaced along the track, while virtually every accessible beach has a campsite nestled amongst forest on foreshore dunes. Most people allow three to five days to walk the 51 kilometres of track between Mārahau in the south and Wainui Bay in the north. Water taxis enable shorter walks for those with less time.

You appreciate almost immediately how much the park differs from all others in New Zealand, simply by the scale of human modification so obvious on the walk from Mārahau over the causeway across Sandy Bay inlet. Here and elsewhere in the park whole hillsides of native forest are recovering from a hundred years of clear-felling and fires—a history of destruction that came to little, largely because the park's soils proved too

OPPOSITE Sand ripples at low tide in Awaroa Inlet

infertile for either plantations or farming. Fortunately, these soil deficiencies meant the devastation of forests never reached its ultimate conclusion. But by the 1930s about three-quarters of the coastal landscape carried the scars of continual burning, and pines, gorse and other introduced weedy plants had spread.

A number of forest reserves already existed, prompting conservationists and community-spirited individuals, most especially the indefatigable Pérrine Moncrieff, to argue for the creation of a national park that combined the reserves with land purchased by government. The national park came to be in December 1942, the beginning of an experiment in landscape recovery in which the hopes of the future lay with the natural regeneration that continues today—along with recent efforts by DOC and volunteers to plant native trees and remove weeds.

Not until turning the first major headland beyond Tinline Bay do you enter a gully and hillside of mature beech forest and experience the splendour of the tall indigenous trees that will, in time, reclothe most of this landscape. To glance through forest windows and see the grey rain-spotted ocean beyond, with Adele Island silently proclaiming a darker-grey presence, is a compelling reason for walking this coastal stretch in the rain. Trees and ferns gleam, and the blackest trunks contrast with subtle variations of iridescent green. Of course rainy weather is clearly not the most favourable for loitering on the beaches that regularly appear after short hillside sidles. These coves are best enjoyed in intense sun when the sky and water are so blue that all other colours except the sands appear subdued and washed of their lustre.

Before the track winds down to the Anchorage Hut and campsite, it cuts over a depauperate hummocky ridge where repeated burnings and virtually non-existent soils have created spasmodic groves of contorted mānuka and kānuka. But even here, as everywhere in the many taller kānuka/mānuka groves

along the track, small native orchids raise their resplendent flowerheads in late spring and summer. From these relatively open heights, a magnificent view opens southward of the waterway known as Astrolabe Roadstead between Adele Island and the bays towards Mārahau. The many French place names come from the navigator Dumont d'Urville, the second European to visit this coast after the Dutch explorer Abel Janszoon Tasman. In marked contrast to Abel Tasman's brief and bloody encounter somewhere off the coast west of Separation Point in 1642, d'Urville and the crew of his corvette *Astrolabe* established close links with Māori during the week they spent hove-to in the roadstead in January 1827. As well as conducting harmonious relations with the local people, d'Urville's visit yielded a valuable historical, scientific and artistic record of the coastline.

From the ridge high above Anchorage, the view north leads through the park's central landscapes: a repeating series of crescent beaches, sandbars, shell-strewn estuaries, coves and headlands. Just as the granite beneath your feet defines the vegetation's limits, when combined with water, granite becomes the main ingredient in the overall shape, colour and texture of the land. The magmatic brew that produced the park's fairly easily weathered 'exfoliating' granite is rich in quartz, feldspar and mica. Large quantities of these sparkling minerals have been eroded into rivers and streams and washed to the coast, where modest currents mass them together to form coarse granite sands ranging in colour from reddish gold to brilliant white. The coastline has evolved into a series of basins carved from more yielding areas of rock between ridges of harder, more resistant rock, resulting in a sequence of curvaceous indentations on an otherwise rugged and irregular coast. A large

OPPOSITE Stream mouth on the beach at Anchorage

Granite rock formations at Watering Cove with Adele Island beyond NICK GROVES

tidal range (three to four metres between high and low tides) adds finishing touches, endlessly rearranging large quantities of colourful sands.

Anchorage Hut is a good base for a day, or at least a morning, exploring the beaches at Torrent Bay, Anchorage and Te Pukatea Bay, the sculpted headlands in between, and the grainy granite blocks sitting incongruously in the river around Cleopatra's Pool, a short walk up the Torrent River. North of Torrent Bay, the Coast Track swings inland for several hours, but retains delightful views into several idyllic estuaries. (After

OPPOSITE Tree ferns line a stream on the Abel Tasman coast

the Falls River swingbridge, it's worth sidling off to Sandfly Bay if you can spare the time.)

Bark Bay, where the next major hut is located, has all the features of the larger estuaries, but on a more intimate scale. A waterfall feeds the lagoon from the northernmost stream, and below its silvery threads you will find a place to sit and contemplate the estuary and beyond. From here the track stretches well inland through a patchy forest of regenerating kānuka and mānuka (also a result of many burn-offs), before regaining the sea at Tonga Quarry (the site of a granite quarry used to furnish stone for a number of prominent buildings and structures in Nelson and Wellington) and the wonderful Onetahuti Beach. Almost certainly somewhere on this sandy shore you'll meet a pair of jet-black oystercatchers strutting confidently on their patch and wishing you a speedy departure up the hill to Awaroa Inlet.

A short stroll from Awaroa Hut leads to the open beach and the cutting where the ocean enters the enormous estuary. Time and again, the sunsets and sunrises visible over Awaroa Bay from the vicinity of this cut are profoundly more affecting than any you'll see on any other Abel Tasman beach. For at least half an hour at either end of a clear summer's day, golden yellow light bathes the estuary's deeply incised sand and shell banks. I suspect the main reason why this place creates such splendid colours and patterns is found in the combination of its east to west aspect, and its dramatic headlands. Almost all the other beaches face north to south, but at Awaroa the sun's rays spread down the beach, with shadows thrown across sand patterns all the more exaggerated by the massive tidal flush that occurs here. Forested headlands at either end of the bay greatly enhance the composition of this scene, forming dark waves that divide the impossibly subtle colours of the sand and sky.

The 13–14 hours between a summer sunrise and sunset at Awaroa can be passed taking long walks down the beach or exploring the estuary at low tide as oystercatchers, white-faced herons and other wading birds feed. On the dunes between beach and estuary you may also find banded dotterel, a small, shy and increasingly threatened bird. Then again, you could pass the time eating cake and drinking real coffee at the Awaroa Lodge café, located at the bay's eastern end.

Having negotiated the route across Awaroa Inlet at low tide, the track north of Awaroa sidles slopes that become increasingly scrubby and modified, until gorse dominates as much as native species. There are, however, some brilliant exceptions to this trend: Goat Bay (reached after 90 minutes) has nīkau palms and sprawling rātā trees that spray red flowerheads onto the beach; Pukatea Walk (another 90 minutes on at Tōtaranui), a short loop track through dense groves of nīkau and tall buttressed pukatea trees; and the arresting muted starkness of the mānuka and kānuka forests beyond the final hut at Whariwharangi Bay (three to four hours from Tōtaranui). The most compelling reason to walk beyond the road at Tōtaranui and along the northeastern corner of the coast to Wainui Inlet (and possibly add another night by staying at the historic homestead hut at Whariwharangi) is to see the granite obelisks at the northern end of Anapai Bay and then head along to Separation Point. For me, the entire journey from Mārahau was worth it for the windy afternoon I spent at Separation Point, watching gannets scorch past cliffs of wrinkled granite, and seals playing with the exuberance of puppies in the wind-tossed seas.

OPPOSITE North Head on the Abel Tasman coast

Early morning light on Tōtaranui Beach PETR HLAVACEK
OPPOSITE Sunrise hits a rock stack on Tōtaranui Beach PETR HLAVACEK
OVERLEAF Dawn colours the sky over Awaroa Inlet

ABEL TASMAN COAST TRACK
Abel Tasman National Park

DISTANCE 51 km
TIME REQUIRED 3–5 days
NEAREST CENTRES Motueka and Tākaka
BEST TIME TO WALK THE TRACK All year
FITNESS Moderate fitness required

The Abel Tasman Coast Track can be walked at any time of the year. In summer months the track is often crowded, however spring, autumn and winter still offer equable weather and walking conditions, with fewer people on the track. During summer months (October to April) bunks at huts must be booked in advance. Hut and camping passes are required. Numerous campsites exist along the route. All huts have toilets, bunks, mattresses and heating, but you will need to take your own cooking equipment. Filtered water supplies are located at all huts and campsites. Good public transport operates to and from the park, with water taxis available to deliver walkers to points along the coast.

APPROXIMATE TRACK TIMES
(south to north):
Mārahau to Anchorage Hut (34 bunks)
11.5 km, 4–5 hours

Anchorage Hut to Bark Bay Hut (34 bunks)
9.5 km, 3–3.5 hours

Bark Bay Hut to Awaroa Hut (22 bunks)
11.5 km, 4–5 hours

Awaroa Hut to Tōtaranui (campsite)
5.5 km, 2–2.5 hours

Tōtaranui to Whariwharangi Hut
(19 bunks)
7.5 km, 3–3.5 hours

Whariwharangi Hut to Wainui carpark
5.5 km, 1.5–2 hours

FURTHER INFORMATION
Nelson Regional Visitor Centre
Millers Acre Centre/Taha o te Awa
79 Trafalgar Street, PO Box 375
Nelson 7010
Tel: 03 546 9339
Email: nelsonvc@doc.govt.nz

Book online at: www.doc.govt.nz
email: greatwalksbooking@doc.govt.nz
or tel: 0800 694 732

TAKAKA

Takaka River

Golden Bay

PIKIKIRUNA RANGE

Wainui Bay

END

carpark

Whariwharangi Hut

Whariwharangi Bay

Tōtaranui

Separation Point

Anapai Bay

Goat Bay

Awaroa Hut

Awaroa Inlet

Falls River

Cleopatra's Pool

Tonga Quarry

Bark Bay Hut

Onetahuti

Anchorage Hut

Torrent Bay

Sandfly Bay

Bark Bay

Tonga Island

Te Pukatea Bay

Tasman Bay

TONGARIRO NORTHERN CIRCUIT

Although many captivating landscapes exist in Tongariro National Park, I would return every year even if there was no more to enjoy than the strange beauty of Red Crater. Found on the highest point of the track, near Mt Tongariro, Red Crater is a deep cloven void those from Hindu cultures would have little difficulty describing as the genital opening, or yoni, which invokes the procreative glory of Mother Earth. Should this metaphor seem risqué, imagine instead an ancient forge still in full heat, blood red and dripping silver metal through the black background. I have walked the lip of this extraordinary structure many times and spiralled down shifting reddy-black pumice into the crater's silent centre of collapsed rocks where strange multicoloured forms blown from the earth carry the pock-marked scars of past eruptions. Surrounded by places where the earth's latent fury steams and regularly explodes from cracks in hot moulded rocks, the centre of Red Crater is a paradox of quiet and peace, a place T.S. Eliot might have called a 'still turning point' or a dynamic centre from which the earth's energy emanates. On the crater's eastern flanks, steam and trickling water from a full-blown geothermal cliff feed a brew of chemicals into three emerald-coloured lakes, and above the pumice and the rainbow hues of scoria on the crater's floor is the strange silver-lipped tongue (the forge within the forge) that dominates the southwestern corner.

Moving about in surreal places like Red Crater, you get the feeling that what was created yesterday could be gone tomorrow, a feeling that is a geological truth on the tramp around the volcanoes of the Tongariro Northern Circuit. Unlike any other long walk in New Zealand, this journey immerses you in a milieu of active volcanoes in which heat from the earth radiates to the surface in ways that are both dramatic and subtle.

I have chosen to describe the route clockwise, beginning from the national park headquarters at Whakapapa Village. After crossing to the Mangatepopo Valley, the track traverses about half of Mt Tongariro's complex slopes, then drops into the Ōturere Valley, where a sidle to Waihohonu Hut ensues. From here, the track swings westward, traversing the saddle that divides Mts Ngāuruhoe and Ruapehu, passing the Tama Lakes and Taranaki Falls before ending back at Whakapapa Village. The full circuit takes three or four days, but those with less time can alternatively tackle the one-day Tongariro Alpine Crossing.

From Whakapapa Village, the first part of your journey follows the well-groomed lower Taranaki Falls Track, before branching off on the Mangatepopo Track at a signposted junction. After crossing the Wairere Stream on a footbridge, the track climbs through the last patch of beech forest you will encounter for more than two days. Devoid of forest, the open terrain here

OPPOSITE Dawn light on Red Crater and Mt Ngāuruhoe BEVAN PERCIVAL

is dissected by many streams, each watercourse deeply etched into the highly erodible volcanic soils. In places, the track has become trench-like, proving that trampers' boots can etch their mark too. Perched on a terrace above the Mangatepopo River is Mangatepopo Hut, which offers a haven from the weather if it is bleak, or—in kinder conditions—provides a fine viewpoint of nearby Mt Tongariro.

The walk up the Mangatepopo Valley is bounded in the south at first by the creamy reddish blocks of lava that make up the huge dome of Pukekaikiore, and then by the immense presence of Mt Ngāuruhoe. On fine days Ngāuruhoe is pitched in perfect symmetry, like a child's tent, black against a blue summer sky, and on stormy days, when all you can glimpse are ascending lines and ridges without apparent end, the mountain seems to take on enormous bulk. The avalanche tracks of knobbly black lava from a 1954 eruption of Ngāuruhoe overlap older grey lava flows. A newer section of track zigzags over these more recent lava flows, crossing the lower flanks of Ngāuruhoe before climbing steadily up to South Crater. South Crater is an eerie plateau of orange–yellow clay, somewhat like a salt lake, where pebbles of pumice and lava have been swirled about in S-curves by rain and snowfall. Large volcanic rocks ejected during violent eruptions lie scattered over the crater floor, and late in summer, blossoming alpine gentians complete a sense of being in a desert.

From here you can climb in long zigzags up Ngāuruhoe, or carry on to Red Crater and circle around to the summit of Tongariro. But with so much to see I wonder about the wisdom of walking too fast and too far in such places. Past Red Crater and down the Ōturere Valley you are still on Tongariro, an old and

OPPOSITE Evening light over Mts Tongariro and Ngāuruhoe
SHAUN BARNETT/BLACK ROBIN PHOTOGRAPHY

Emerald Lake, Mt Tongariro
OPPOSITE Mts Ngāuruhoe and Tongariro, coated with snow-covered ash after a Mt Ruapehu eruption

spacious monarch who lords it over the landscape, his impressive girth bedecked with exquisite jewels and other finery: the perfect circles of Blue and Emerald lakes, the Te Maari craters, Ketetahi Hot Springs and the South, North and Red craters. Trampers were once again reminded of the explosive nature of this volcanic environment when the Te Maari craters erupted twice in 2012. Although both were minor eruptions, one was sufficiently violent to spew an ash plume six kilometres into the air, and catapult boulders far enough to destroy Ketetahi Hut—resulting in the closure of the Tongariro Alpine Crossing for some weeks.

Although it's hard to tear yourself away from the centre of Tongariro, the walk down twisting sheets of lava and across the Ōturere Valley to Ōturere Hut should not be rushed. One reason is to allow time among the strange statue-like blocks that litter the valley's sandy plain, a collection of eccentric lava structures seemingly 'frozen' into shape because they cooled so rapidly.

From Ōturere Hut the journey to Waihohonu Hut crosses dry, open terrain, pock-marked by boulders, past lava flows and mosaics of scrub and skirting through clumps of beech forest. Occasionally, the scrub retreats into defensive circles, rather like threatened wagon trains. On the outer margins is a protective golden palisade of miniature tōtara trees just 15 centimetres high, then a rank of grey *Rhacomitrium* moss, and massed in the centre are *Dracophyllum*, tall hebes and the occasional mountain toatoa.

A rise, just before the descent to Waihohonu Hut, offers a view of the Rangipō Desert, with its sweeps of eroded and deeply gullied ash and pumice, and high ridges stretching through the landscape like long ochre limbs.

Six months after Mt Ruapehu erupted in July 1996, much of the area was covered in a taut grey skin of waterlogged ash

that cracked and emitted a stinking sulphurous smell from under my feet as I walked along. This of course is part of the central story of the park, in which the earth has erupted and turned itself inside out many times, though no one has ever witnessed the terrifying scale and force of the largest eruptions that have occurred over the past hundreds of thousands of years. Though spectacular, the more recent eruptions were an extremely minor episode in a long and violent geological history. Numerous volcanoes have stood on this landscape, and Ruapehu and Tongariro are simply the latest of these, relatively young (20,000 years) 'strato-volcanoes' comprised of composite cones and multiple layers of ash, scoria and lava.

Waihohonu Hut is the newest and largest in the national park; architecturally designed with a large living area and two huge windows, each angled perfectly to frame views of either Ruapehu or Ngāuruhoe. It's the third hut to have existed in the area, each built by successive government departments. The Department of Conservation built the current hut in 2010, which replaced an earlier hut built in 1968 (since removed), during the era when the Department of Lands and Survey managed the park.

The original hut still exists, nestled in a small clearing among beech trees about 10 minutes' walk from the new hut. Now called the 'Old Waihohonu Hut', it was built over the summer of 1903–04 by the Department of Tourism and Resorts, when the newly created agency was keen to develop infrastructure in the country's scenic hotspots, including Tongariro. In keeping with the social etiquette of the times, the hut had two rooms, so the sexes could be separated at night. While the men occupied the larger room, which had an open fire, the women

OPPOSITE On the edge of Tongariro's Red Crater, looking north across the Emerald Lakes towards Blue Lake

The historic Old Waihohonu Hut, built in 1903–4 SHAUN BARNETT/BLACK ROBIN PHOTOGRAPHY

got the colder, smaller room. Clad in corrugated iron, the hut was—appropriately enough—insulated using locally sourced pumice jammed into the walls. However, despite the insulation, the hut could be bitterly cold in winter, with the supplied blankets hardly up to the task of keeping the occupants warm. No doubt women occasionally chose to stay in the fire-warmed men's room, with practicality overruling any moral obligations.

For a few years, skiers and climbers were the main users of the hut, which served as a good base for forays up Te Heuheu on Ruapehu's northern flanks. Collectively the three huts have spanned over 110 years of mountain accommodation in the park.

Your final day traverses the often barren country of Tama Saddle, with Ruapehu—from this angle shaped like an upturned ship's prow—on one side, and the symmetrical cone of Ngāuruhoe on the other. The well-poled route follows the course of the burbling Waihohonu River at first, before beginning a gradual climb to the saddle.

A signposted junction marks the track to the Tama Lakes—a worthwhile side trip if the weather remains conducive. Both are sizeable, startlingly blue alpine lakes, lying in explosion craters formed from relatively recent volcanic activity. The viewpoint over the Lower Tama Lake is only 15 minutes from

The Emerald Lakes on the descent from Red Crater PETR HLAVACEK

Mt Ruapehu at sunrise from the Waihohonu Track SHAUN BARNETT/BLACK ROBIN PHOTOGRAPHY

the main track, while reaching the vantage point of the Upper Tama Lake, the deeper and larger of the two, takes about 45 minutes' walking. On a good day, the ridge overlooking the lake provides a commanding viewpoint, and grand location to eat lunch.

Back at Tama Saddle, the marker poles lead gradually downward, across soft, easily eroded volcanic soils. En route, squat plants like the red and sharply leaved *Dracophyllum recurvum*, small white-flowering foxgloves and the North Island eyebright assert their life and colours. At Taranaki Falls, the colours of the land become even stronger, when mountain beech trees draped in white lichen enfold you in their comforting greenness for the first time in two days.

It's worth taking the stairs down to the base of the falls, where the Wairere River plunges 20 metres over a steep escarpment created by an old lava flow. It's possible to scramble around the pool at the base of the falls, and creep in behind the tumbling water—if you don't mind getting wet.

The main track to Whakapapa Village, now only an hour away, is well graded and gravelled. After crossing the footbridge above the falls, the track leads across alpine tussock and shrublands, with the Chateau Tongariro becoming increasingly prominent as you draw near. This large hotel, modelled on those constructed in the Canadian Rockies, was built in the 1930s. While grand, from this angle it is suitably dwarfed by Ruapehu, one of the world's most active volcanoes.

—*Shaun Barnett*

OPPOSITE Trampers on the Ōturere Track, with Mt Ngāuruhoe in cloud
SHAUN BARNETT/BLACK ROBIN PHOTOGRAPHY

TONGARIRO NORTHERN CIRCUIT

Tongariro National Park

DISTANCE 42 km

TIME REQUIRED 3–4 days

NEAREST CENTRE Whakapapa Village

BEST TIME TO WALK THE TRACK
November–April

FITNESS Moderate fitness required

BOOKING All huts and campsites must be booked in advance

The Tongariro Northern Circuit is a varied forest and alpine walk through a range of volcanic landforms along well-marked, though often quite exposed, tracks. In bad weather, sections of this route (in particular Red Crater and Tama Saddle) may be impossible due to rain, poor visibility or snow. Good equipment and boots are essential. Huts have bunks, wood stoves for heating, gas cookers, a water supply and toilets. Campsites exist near all three huts at Mangatepopo, Ōturere and Waihohonu. In the peak season between October and April, all campsites and huts must be booked well in advance. Whakapapa Village on the northern slopes of Mt Ruapehu has accommodation ranging from campsites to luxury accommodation, visitor information and a general store. Shuttle services can be arranged for those wanting to be dropped off at points around the park.

APPROXIMATE TRACK TIMES
(clockwise direction):

Whakapapa Village to Mangatepopo Hut
(23 bunks)
8.5 km, 3–4 hours

Mangatepopo Hut to Ōturere Hut
(26 bunks)
10.3 km, 5–6 hours

Ōturere Hut to Waihohonu Hut (29 bunks)
8.5 km, 3 hours

Waihohonu Hut to Whakapapa Village via Tama Saddle
14.3 km, 5–6 hours

Side-trip from Tama Saddle to Lower Tama Lake
30 minutes return

To Upper Tama Lake
1.5 hours return

FURTHER INFORMATION
Tongariro National Park Visitor Centre
Department of Conservation
State Highway 48, Whakapapa Village
PO Box 71029, Mt Ruapehu 3951
Tel: 07 892 3729
Email: tongarirovc@doc.govt.nz

Book online at: www.doc.govt.nz
email: greatwalksbooking@doc.govt.nz
or tel: 0800 694 732

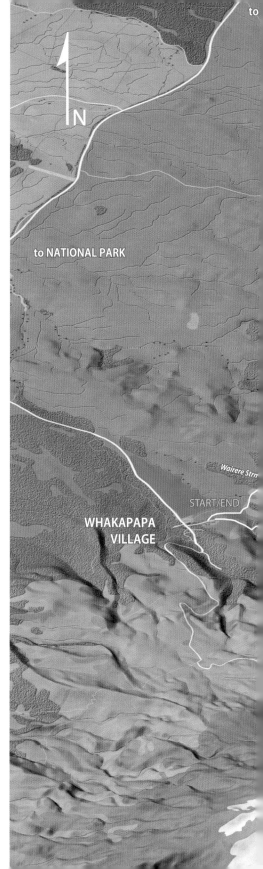

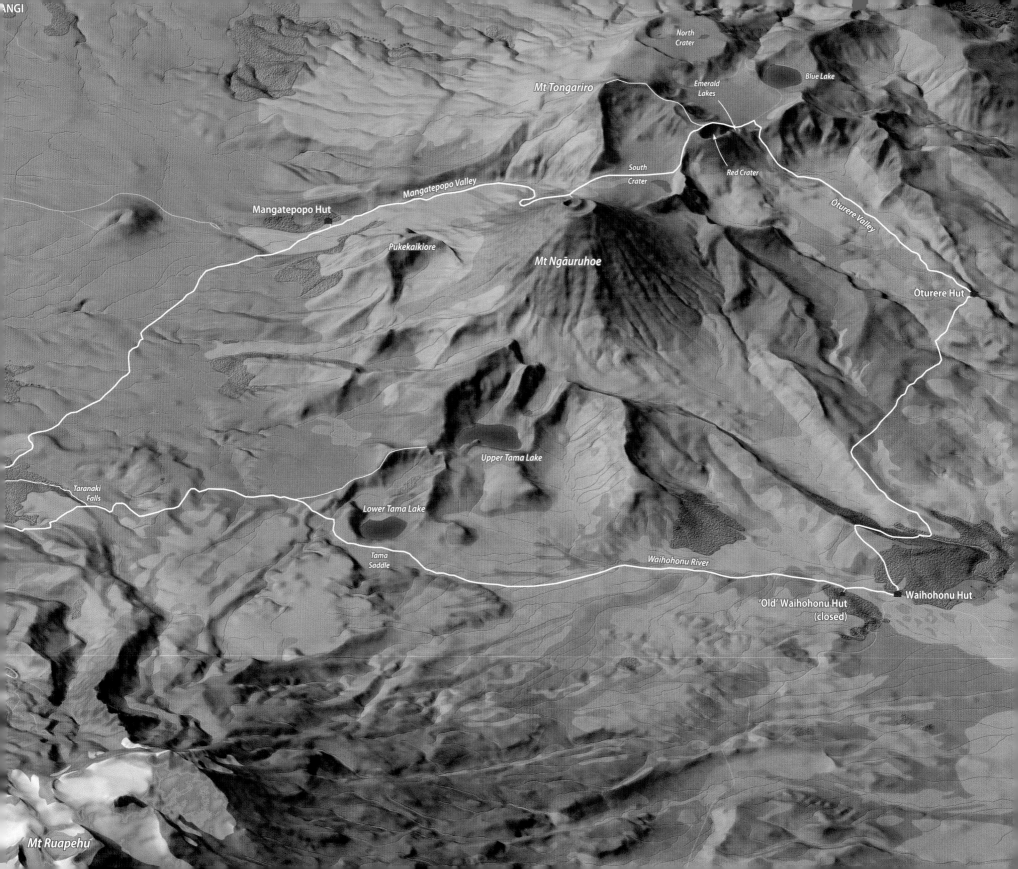

ANGI

North Crater

Mt Tongariro

Emerald Lakes

Blue Lake

South Crater

Red Crater

Ōturere Valley

Mangatepopo Valley

Mangatepopo Hut

Pukekaikiore

Mt Ngāuruhoe

Ōturere Hut

Upper Tama Lake

Taranaki Falls

Lower Tama Lake

Tama Saddle

Waihohonu River

'Old' Waihohonu Hut (closed)

Waihohonu Hut

Mt Ruapehu

LAKE WAIKAREMOANA TRACK

Despite the dusty road that splits the huge Te Urewera wilderness, there remains a sense of 'other-worldliness' about these heavily forested ranges. In this largest of all the fragments of North Island forest, the author Katherine Mansfield also sensed a mood when she wrote 'it is all so gigantic and tragic—and even in the bright sunlight it is so passionately secret.' Ngāi Tūhoe and neighbouring iwi, who lived in these ranges for hundreds of years before Pākehā arrived, discovered its hallowed places and secrets, and named its rivers, lakes, forests and mountain ranges. So powerfully does the land speak, that Tūhoe trace their ancestry to the coupling of the mist maiden Hine-pūkohu-rangi and the mountain Te Maunga, a myth from which comes the name 'Children of the Mist', as Tūhoe are also known. Tūhoe alone can recount these mysteries should you wish to discover more about them, though glimpses of their relationship with the land are revealed in Elsdon Best's monographs on the Tūhoe and Judith Binney's works on Tūhoe prophets Rua Kēnana and Te Kooti. But, better still, if chance or grace allows it, speak directly to and learn from the Tūhoe, who still live near the sacred centres of their land. No matter from where our myths and unconscious calls emanate, Lake Waikaremoana and Te Urewera's forests have a deep resonance for all who visit them.

Many now make the journey around Lake Waikaremoana, which from on high appears gangly and long-fingered, an aquamarine starfish held by an enveloping clasp of forest. The popular myth describing the lake's creation tells the tragic story of Haumapuhia, a woman whose defiance towards her father so angered him that he decided to drown her. Struggling desperately against her father, she called for mercy from the Gods. They transformed her into a taniwha, and she desperately thrashed through the land, gouging the enclosing hillsides in her attempts to find an escape to the ocean. Water filled the places where she clawed at the hillsides and the lake was created, and although Haumapuhia lost her struggle when daylight came and turned her to stone, the lake's many bays and indentations are reminders of her tragic struggle. Certainly the land offers no easy ways to orientate and get one's bearings because no single mountain peak rises above the forest and no central river dominates; it's just a series of sharp ridges and deep valleys, one upon another, spiralling out from the lake. In fact the only interruption from the forest blanket is Panekiri Bluff, the severe rock escarpment on the lake's southern shores.

Panekiri Bluff rises 600 metres from the lake, its great walls glowing a golden pallor on sunny days, and wreathed in mist and cloud when it rains. Perched high on these bluffs sits Panekiri

OPPOSITE Lake Waikaremoana from Panekiri Bluff
OVERLEAF Sunrise on Panekiri Bluff and Lake Waikaremoana
BEVAN PERCIVAL

Hut, a grand viewpoint over a superb wilderness. For some it is near the end, and for others just the start of their circumnavigation of Waikaremoana. Below lies the lake and a view of water and forest ridges overlapping blue on blue, while beyond, more ethereal blues denote ridges westward to the horizon. I once stood outside looking west when a German backpacker interrupted my quiet with the simple truism: 'everywhere you look is forest'. In the peace of such high places, where no water runs except for the rain and the mist gathering on trees, and no sound disturbs except the tuneless whistling of the wind, you can look upon a view without the imprint of human interference and find spoken works remarkably unnecessary.

Because many people look at Panekiri Bluff seduced by the prospects of wonderful morning and evening views (and perhaps fearful of the hard grunt from the lake to the top) they set out to walk Waikaremoana clockwise, as most guidebooks suggest. However there is no method to the madness of walking straight up a bluff on the first day. It is much better to engage a shuttle bus or water taxi to the Hopuruahine entrance and take on the hill-climb on the last day after you have eaten your way through some of your pack's load and worked a few muscles into shape.

The Lake Waikaremoana Track is a 46-kilometre-long trail, largely in excellent condition, that can be dawdled in five days and easily tramped in four. From the Hopuruahine entrance, the first five hours between Whanganui Hut and Tapuaenui Campsite to the large new Waiharuru Hut introduce you to the three types of forest that you'll encounter off and on over the next few days: a resplendent mature rimu–tawa forest, largely in the gullies; regenerating mānuka–tree fern patches, usually closer to the water's edge (resulting from new surfaces exposed in 1946 when hydro development lowered the lake's level by five metres), and on the drier ridges and faces, the more open sooty-barked hard beech and mingimingi forest. The diverse forest boasts some wonderfully buttressed beech trees, and perhaps because of its overall size and variety and the insects that gather over the water's edge, seems particularly rich in birdlife. Unless you're unlucky, you'll hear and see kākā and kākāriki and, at night, hear moreporks calling dolefully for 'more pork', and screeching North Island brown kiwi. Common birds are abundant: wood pigeons, paradise ducks, whiteheads, riflemen, grey warblers, tomtits, fantails and silvereyes. What you almost definitely won't see (and won't be sensitive enough to hear) are the rare nocturnal long-tailed and short-tailed bats that roost in the boles of ancient trees.

Marauiti Hut, three hours' walk from Waiharuru Hut, is pleasantly sited beside a finger of water where the broad Marauiti River flows gently into the lake at Marauiti Bay. The hut's red roof and expansive cream lounge with large windows is a convivial place even on the greyest of days, and if the mosquitoes and sandflies aren't too bad, its sheltered porch provides a good place for taking in the view while contemplating dinner.

The track beyond Marauiti heads over a beech-covered spur with strongly buttressed trees, along with many tawa and a few scattered rimu. Then it leads down into one of Waikaremoana's typically small and grassy lakeside flats, this one at Maraunui Bay. Here there are groves of mānuka and grassy banks beside the creek and lakeside. A virtue of this walk for those who find fitness a challenge is that no stretch is too long before you happen upon a place where you can quietly meditate upon the view and rest tired muscles. And in such vein, although it may seem like an unnecessary uphill diversion late in the afternoon, you should take the side track up to Korokoro Falls, which

OPPOSITE Sunlight filtering through beech forest on the Lake Waikaremoana Track STEFAN MARKS

114

Marauiti Hut on the shore of Marauiti Bay
OPPOSITE Korokoro Falls, a short distance up Korokorowhaitiri Stream from the lake track

Morning mist at Marauiti Bay, Lake Waikaremoana SHAUN BARNETT/BLACK ROBIN PHOTOGRAPHY

are definitely worth the effort. An enchanting ridge track leads through a lush forest of tānekaha, the large-leaved mountain neinei and stunted forms of beech trees standing out from the dense, twirling groves of tawa. Below the track Te Korokorowhaitiri Stream gives sculptural expression to blocks of limestone that have been progressively rolled down the creek bed.

The smallish stream won't prepare you for the size of the waterfall, which is sighted through an envelope of large beech trees rising from a carpet of kidney ferns. In rain, water fills the face of the fall, forming a rectangular 20-metre-high curtain of water. By climbing carefully down on the left (when you look towards the falls), you can walk on a scalloped, gently sloping papa (mudstone) shelf among several huge boulders—sentinels to the falls themselves. Because papa is so consistent in constitution, and so water-soluble, it erodes like limestone, leaving sculpted blocks of harder rocks resting on flat surfaces and weir-like drops covered with gentle flows of water.

The next day's climb from Waiopaoa to Panekiri Hut follows a series of obvious ridge lines for the first two hours, before zigzagging between bluffs to gain the Panekiri Range, and then the hut after a further hour-and-a-half of easy wandering. From above the zigzag, silver beech gives way to mountain beech, and mountain tōtara replaces tawa as the dominant understorey trees. On these steeper slopes the long plank-like black buttresses of beech trees form sheets that slice into the dark earth. Misty clouds often cover the range, even when the weather is clear below. It is at these times that the mosses and lichen blanketing the trees and branches stand out in swollen clumps, giving the impression that every tree is ancient.

After an evening and early morning at Panekiri Hut, the route down the Panekiri Range to complete the track at the road end is essentially a reversal of the day before, starting with the 'ancient' mist forest and descending through tawa

Tawa forest beside Lake Waikaremoana

groves to the great lake. Several lookouts on this descent not only give magnificent views, but also lead your thoughts back 2200 years when a huge landslip detached from the Ngamoko Range (north of the lake's exit) and blocked the Waikaretāheke River, allowing the waters of Waikaremoana to fill up. This is the geological explanation of Waikaremoana, a story that, like Māori myths and the Pākehā's sense of mystery, lies hidden under a forest mantle, but which still reverberates in the unconscious like a passionate secret.

LAKE WAIKAREMOANA TRACK
Te Urewera

DISTANCE 46 km

TIME REQUIRED 3–4 days

NEAREST TOWN Wairoa

BEST TIME TO WALK THE TRACK
September–May

FITNESS Moderate fitness required

The Lake Waikaremoana Track is well constructed and has several large huts supplied with bunks and mattresses. Some also have heating. You need to take your own cooking equipment. Several campsites exist along the track though camping is not permitted on the Panekiri Range (including next to Panekiri Hut). Hut and camping passes are required, and must be booked all year round. The track can be reached on State Highway 38, either from Wairoa in the east, or from Murupara and Rotorua west of the lake. Bus transport operates over State Highway 38.

APPROXIMATE WALKING TIMES
(anticlockwise direction from Hopuruahine track entrance):

Hopuruahine Landing to Whanganui Hut
(18 bunks)
2.7 km, 1 hour

Whanganui Hut to Waiharuru Hut
(40 bunks)
6.5 km, 2 hours

Waiharuru Hut to Marauiti Hut
(26 bunks)
6.5 km, 2 hours

Marauiti Hut to Waiopaoa Hut
(30 bunks)
12 km, 4.5–5 hours

Waiopaoa Hut to Panekiri Hut
(36 bunks)
8 km, 3–4 hours

Panekiri Hut to Onepoto track entrance
9 km, 4–6 hours

FURTHER INFORMATION
Te Urewera Visitor Centre
House 2 Aniwaniwa
State Highway 38,
Te Urewera 4195
Tel: 06 837 3803
Email: teureweravc@doc.govt.nz

Book online at: www.doc.govt.nz
email: greatwalksbooking@doc.govt.nz
or tel: 0800 694 732

to MURUPARA

START
Hopuruahine
Landing

Whanganui Hut

Tapuaenui

Waiharuru Hut

Whanganui Inlet

Lake
Waikareiti

ANIWANIWA

WAIKAREMOANA

rauiti Bay

i Bay

Wairaumoana (Wairau Arm)

Lake Waikaremoana

NGAMOKO RANGE

Panekiri Bluff

Panekiri Hut

END   Onepoto

to WAIROA

TRAMPING IN NEW ZEALAND

The eight Great Walks described in this book are maintained by the Department of Conservation (DOC). All are well-constructed tracks that are easy to follow, with major obstacles like rivers safely bridged and generally provide a higher standard of facilities than most other tracks in New Zealand. Due to their popularity, all Great Walks huts must be booked in advance during the peak summer season, and for some of the tracks, all year round (see: www.greatwalks.co.nz). Fees for staying in huts vary according to the Great Walk, but range from $32 to $54. Huts are free for children and youths under 18, but must still be booked in advance.

Many of the tracks have designated campsites, which also must be booked in advance. Camping is not permitted near the track except at these designated sites. On some of the walks you will need to carry your own cooking equipment and utensils, and even where gas is supplied for cooking, having your own cooker will mean an early dinner in a crowded hut. A variety of companies offer guided walks on most of the Great Walks, and there are private huts on the Milford, Routeburn and Abel Tasman tracks.

When should you go? The summer months, between December and March, are obviously the best because of the warmer temperatures, longer daylight hours and generally drier conditions underfoot. But spring and autumn can also provide good walking conditions, and there are often fewer people on the tracks. For several months during winter, the Kepler, Milford and Routeburn tracks may be impassable because of snow or high avalanche danger. The Heaphy Track is occasionally closed by snow but is often walked in winter. The Tongariro Northern Circuit is subject to some snow on higher sections and is often a marginal winter walk. However, the Abel Tasman Coast Track and Lake Waikaremoana Track are both feasible through winter months, and although the nights may be cold, daytime temperatures can be pleasantly mild.

The success of your walk will hinge on your preparation—being physically fit and able to carry a pack, your route research, having appropriate equipment and being prepared for bad weather or accidents. Talk to others who have done the walk. Get up-to-date information about track conditions from DOC staff, visitor centres or by searching online. DOC has brochures available to download for all Great Walks, and there are many tramping guidebooks that provide more information than is possible in a book of this nature.

One of the most unpredictable factors in the backcountry is the weather. All of these routes are susceptible to bad weather, flooded rivers, slips, snow and high winds. Although all major rivers are bridged on the Great Walks described in this book, during exceptionally wet weather, tiny side-streams can flood and become impossible to ford. If in doubt, back off and retreat to the last hut.

To be prepared for the inevitable downpour, good storm clothing and strong footwear is essential for all these walks. 'Reading' weather in the mountains comes with experience, but perhaps the soundest advice is to be conservative in your decision-making about whether to carry on. Listen to the advice of hut wardens and other walkers, and if you are out in bad weather, be wary of hypothermia among members of your party (hypothermia is a dangerous cooling of the core body temperature that can occur with little warning during exposure to cold weather and, if untreated, leads to death).

Don't forget to take a sunhat, and carry sunscreen and insect repellent in your first aid kit—and leave intentions of your trip with a reliable friend.

RECOMMENDED READING

Barnett, Shaun, *Tramping in New Zealand*, Potton & Burton, Nelson, 2015 (second edition).

Barnett, Shaun, *Day Walks in New Zealand*, Craig Potton Publishing, Nelson, 2007.

Barnett, Shaun & Chris Maclean, *Tramping: A New Zealand history*, Craig Potton Publishing, Nelson, revised edition 2015.

Barnett, Shaun, Rob Brown & Geoff Spearpoint, *Shelter from the Storm: The story of New Zealand's backcountry huts*, Craig Potton Publishing, Nelson, 2012.

Bennett, Sarah & Lee Slater, The *New Zealand Trampers' Handbook*, Craig Potton Publishing, Nelson, 2010.

Brown, Rob, *Rakiura: The wilderness of Stewart Island*, Craig Potton Publishing, Nelson, 2006.

Dawson, John & Rob Lucas, *Nature Guide to the New Zealand Forest*, Godwit, Auckland, 2000.

Dawson, John & Rob Lucas, *Field Guide to New Zealand's Native Trees*, Craig Potton Publishing, Nelson, 2012.

Forsyth, J, I. Turnbull, B. Lee & G. Beecroft, *A Guide to the Kepler Track*, John McIndoe in association with DSIR, Dunedin, 1991.

Gibbs, George, *Ghosts of Gondwana: The history of life in New Zealand*, Craig Potton Publishing, Nelson, 2006.

Hall-Jones, John, *Stewart Island Explored*, Craig Printing, Invercargill, 1994.

Heather, Barrie & Hugh Robertson, *The Field Guide to the Birds of New Zealand*, Penguin, Auckland, revised edition 2015.

Mark, Alan F., *Above the Treeline: A nature guide to alpine New Zealand*, Craig Potton Publishing, Nelson, 2012.

Molloy, Les & Roger Smith, *Landforms: The shaping of New Zealand*, Craig Potton Publishing, Nelson, 2002.

Molloy, Les & Craig Potton, *New Zealand's Wilderness Heritage*, Craig Potton Publishing, Nelson, 2014 (second edition).

Natusch, Sheila, *Stewart Island: A souvenir*, Craig Printing, Invercargill, 1983.

Ombler, Kathy, *A Visitor's Guide to New Zealand National Parks*, New Holland, Auckland, 2005.

Petyt, Chris, *The Heaphy Track*, Nikau Press, Nelson, 2012.

Sansom, Olga, *In the Grip of an Island: Early Stewart Island history*, Craig Printing, Invercargill, 1982.

Thornton, J., *Field Guide to New Zealand Geology*. Reed Methuen, Auckland, 1985.

Young, David, *Our Islands, Our Selves: A history of conservation in New Zealand*, Otago University Press, Dunedin, 2004.

Published by Potton & Burton, PO Box 5128, Nelson, New Zealand

©2015 Craig Potton and Shaun Barnett

Text: Craig Potton and Shaun Barnett
Photographs: Craig Potton, and individual photographers as credited
Printing: Midas Printing International Ltd, China

ISBN 978 1 927213 63 6